CONTENTS

THANKS AND THANKS AGAIN!

This project is definitely a team effort. First of all, thank you to Cathy, Christy, Rebecca and Heidi Burns, the women of my life.

Thank you to Jill Corey, my incredible assistant and longtime friend.

Thank you to Doug Webster for your outstanding job as executive director of the National Institute of Youth Ministry (NIYM).

Thank you to the NIYM staff in San Clemente: Gary Lenhart, Russ Cline, Laurie Pilz, Luchi Bierbower, Dean Bruns and Larry Acosta.

Thank you to our 100-plus associate trainers who have been my coworkers, friends and sacrificial guinea pigs.

Thank you to Kyle Duncan, Bill Greig III and Jean Daly for convincing me that Gospel Light is a great publisher that deeply believes in the mission to reach young people. I believe!

Thank you to the Youth Specialties world. Tic, Mike and Wayne, so many years ago, you brought on a wet-behind-the-ears youth worker with hair and taught me most everything I know about youth work today.

Thank you to the hundreds of donors, supporters and friends of NIYM. You are helping create an international grassroots movement that is helping young people make positive decisions that will affect them for the rest of their lives.

"Where there is no counsel, the people fall; But in the multitude of counselors there is safety"
(Proverbs 11:14, *NKJV*).

Jim Burns
San Clemente, CA

DEDICATION

To Gary and Debbie Lenhart
From youth-group kids to coworkers and two of my most treasured friends:

You are an inspiration.
You are real.
Your faith shines.

THE **W**ORD ON HELPING FRIENDS IN CRISIS

JIM BURNS

THE NATIONAL INSTITUTE OF YOUTH MINISTRY

Gospel Light

Gospel Light is an evangelical Christian publisher dedicated to serving the local church. We believe God's vision for Gospel Light is to provide church leaders with biblical, user-friendly materials that will help them evangelize, disciple and minister to children, youth and families.

We hope this Gospel Light resource will help you discover biblical truth for your own life and help you minister to youth. God bless you in your work.

For a free catalog of resources from Gospel Light please contact your Christian supplier or call 1-800-4-GOSPEL.

PUBLISHING STAFF

Jean Daly, Editor
Pam Weston, Editorial Assistant
Kyle Duncan, Editorial Director
Bayard Taylor, M. Div., Editor, Theological and Biblical Issues
Joey O'Connor, Contributing Writer
Mario Ricketts, Designer

HOW TO MAKE CLEAN COPIES FROM THIS BOOK

YOU MAY MAKE COPIES OF PORTIONS OF THIS BOOK WITH A CLEAN CONSCIENCE IF:

- you (or someone in your organization) are the original purchaser;
- you are using the copies you make for a noncommercial purpose (such as teaching or promoting your ministry) within your church or organization;
- you follow the instructions provided in this book.

HOWEVER, IT IS ILLEGAL FOR YOU TO MAKE COPIES IF:

- you are using the material to promote, advertise or sell a product or service other than for ministry fund-raising;
- you are using the material in or on a product for sale;
- you or your organization are not the original purchaser of this book.

By following these guidelines you help us keep our products affordable.

Thank you,

Gospel Light

PRAISE FOR YOUTHBUILDERS

Jim Burns knows young people. He also knows how to communicate to them. This study should be in the hands of every youth leader interested in discipling young people.

David Adams, Vice President, Lexington Baptist College

I deeply respect and appreciate the groundwork Jim Burns has prepared for true teenage discernment. YouthBuilders is timeless in the sense that the framework has made it possible to plug into any society, at any point in time, and to proceed to discuss, experience and arrive at sincere moral and Christian conclusions that will lead to growth and life changes. Reaching young people may be more difficult today than ever before, but God's grace is alive and well in Jim Burns and this wonderful curriculum.

Fr. Angelo J. Artemas, Youth Ministry Director, Greek Orthodox Archdiocese of North and South America

I heartily recommend Jim Burns's *YouthBuilders Group Bible Studies* because they are leader-friendly tools that are ready to use in youth groups and Sunday School classes. Jim addresses the tough questions that students are genuinely facing every day and, through his engaging style, challenges young people to make their own decisions to move from their current opinions to God's convictions taught in the Bible. Every youth group will benefit from this excellent curriculum.

Paul Borthwick, Minister of Missions, Grace Chapel

Jim Burns recognizes the fact that small groups are where life change happens. In this study he has captured the essence of that value. Further, Jim has given much thought to shaping this very effective material into a usable tool that serves the parent, leader and student.

Bo Boshers, Executive Director, Student Impact,
Willow Creek Community Church

It is about time that someone who knows kids, understands kids and works with kids writes youth curriculum that youth workers, both volunteer and professional, can use. Jim Burns's *YouthBuilders Group Bible Studies* is the curriculum that youth ministry has been waiting a long time for.

Ridge Burns, President,
The Center for Student Missions

There are very few people in the world who know how to communicate life-changing truth effectively to teens. Jim Burns is one of the best. *YouthBuilders Group Bible Studies* puts handles on those skills and makes them available to everyone. These studies are biblically sound, hands-on practical and just plain fun. This one gets a five-star endorsement—which isn't bad since there are only four stars to start with.

Ken Davis, President,
Dynamic Communications

I don't know anyone who knows and understands the needs of the youth worker like Jim Burns. His new curriculum not only reveals his knowledge of youth ministry but also his depth and sensitivity to the Scriptures. *YouthBuilders Group Bible Studies* is solid, easy to use and gets students out of their seats and into the Word. I've been waiting for something like this for a long time!

Doug Fields, Pastor of High School,
Saddleback Valley Community Church

Jim Burns has a way of being creative without being "hokey." *YouthBuilders Group Bible Studies* takes the age-old model of curriculum and gives it a new look with tools such as the Bible *Tuck-In*™ and Parent Page. Give this new resource a try and you'll see that Jim shoots straightforward on tough issues. The *YouthBuilders* series is great for leading small-group discussions as well as teaching a large class of junior high or high school students. The Parent Page will help you get support from your parents in that they will understand the topics you

are dealing with in your group. Put Jim's years of experience to work for you by equipping yourself with this quality material.

Curt Gibson, Pastor to Junior High,
First Church of the Nazarene of Pasadena

Once again, Jim Burns has managed to handle very timely issues with just the right touch. His *YouthBuilders Group Bible Studies* succeeds in teaching solid biblical values without being stuffy or preachy. The format is user-friendly, designed to stimulate high involvement and deep discussion. Especially impressive is the Parent Page, a long overdue tool to help parents become part of the Christian education loop. I look forward to using it with my kids!

David M. Hughes, Pastor,
First Baptist Church, Winston-Salem

What do you get when you combine a deep love for teens, over 20 years' experience in youth ministry and an excellent writer? You get Jim Burns's *YouthBuilders* series! This stuff has absolutely hit the nail on the head. Quality Sunday School and small-group material is tough to come by these days, but Jim has put every ounce of creativity he has into these books.

Greg Johnson, author of *Getting Ready for the Guy/Girl Thing* and *Keeping Your Cool While Sharing Your Faith*

Jim Burns has a gift, the gift of combining the relational and theological dynamics of our faith in a graceful, relevant and easy-to-chew-and-swallow way. *YouthBuilders Group Bible Studies* is a hit, not only for teens but for teachers.

Gregg Johnson, National Youth Director,
International Church of the Foursquare Gospel

The practicing youth worker always needs more ammunition. Here is a whole book full of practical, usable resources for those facing kids face-to-face. *YouthBuilders Group Bible Studies* will get that blank stare off the faces of kids in your youth meeting!
Jay Kesler, President, Taylor University

I couldn't be more excited about the *YouthBuilders Group Bible Studies*. It couldn't have arrived at a more needed time. Spiritually we approach the future engaged in war with young people taking direct hits from the devil. This series will practically help teens who feel partially equipped to "put on the whole armor of God."
Mike MacIntosh, Pastor,
Horizon Christian Fellowship

In *YouthBuilders Group Bible Studies*, Jim Burns pulls together the key ingredients for an effective curriculum series. Jim captures the combination of teen involvement and a solid biblical perspective, with topics that are relevant and straightforward. This series will be a valuable tool in the local church.
Dennis "Tiger" McLuen, Executive Director,
Youth Leadership

My ministry takes me to the lost kids in our nation's cities where youth games and activities are often irrelevant and plain Bible knowledge for the sake of learning is unattractive. Young people need the information necessary to make wise decisions related to everyday problems. *YouthBuilders* will help many young people integrate their faith into everyday life, which after all is our goal as youth workers.
Miles McPherson, President, Project Intercept

Jim Burns's passion for teens, youth workers and parents of teens is evident in the *YouthBuilders Group Bible Studies*. He has a gift of presenting biblical truths on a

level teens will fully understand, and youth workers and parents can easily communicate.
Al Menconi, President, Al Menconi Ministries

Youth ministry curriculum is often directed to only one spoke of the wheel of youth ministry—the adolescent. Not so with this material! Jim has enlarged the education circle, including information for the adolescent, the parent and the youth worker. *YouthBuilders Group Bible Studies* is youth and family ministry-oriented material at its best.
Helen Musick, Instructor of Youth Ministry,
Asbury Seminary

Finally, a Bible study that has it all! It's action-packed, practical and biblical; but that's only the beginning. *YouthBuilders* involves students in the Scriptures. It's relational, interactive and leads kids toward lifestyle changes. The unique aspect is a page for parents, something that's usually missing from adolescent curriculum. Jim Burns has outdone himself. This isn't a home run—it's a grand slam!
Dr. David Olshine, Director of Youth Ministries,
Columbia International University

Here is a thoughtful and relevant curriculum designed to meet the needs of youth workers, parents and students. It's creative, interactive and biblical—and with Jim Burns's name on it, you know you're getting a quality resource.
Laurie Polich, Youth Director,
First Presbyterian Church of Berkeley

In 10 years of youth ministry I've never used a curriculum because I've never found anything that actively involves students in the learning process, speaks to young people where they are and challenges them with biblical truth—I'll use this! *YouthBuilders Group Bible Studies* is a complete curriculum that is helpful to parents, youth leaders and, most importantly, today's youth.

Glenn Schroeder, Youth and Young Adult Ministries, Vineyard Christian Fellowship, Anaheim

This new material by Jim Burns represents a vitality in curriculum and, I believe, a more mature and faithful direction. *YouthBuilders Group Bible Studies* challenges youth by teaching them how to make decisions rather than telling them what decisions to make. Each session offers teaching concepts, presents options and asks for a decision. I believe it's healthy, the way Christ taught and represents the abilities, personhood and faithfulness of youth. I give it an A+!

J. David Stone, President, Stone & Associates

Jim Burns has done it again! This is a practical, timely and reality-based resource for equipping teens to live life in the fast-paced, pressure-packed adolescent world of the '90s. A very refreshing creative oasis in the curriculum desert!

Rich Van Pelt, President, Alongside Ministries

YouthBuilders Group Bible Studies is a tremendous new set of resources for reaching students. Jim has his finger on the pulse of youth today. He understands their mind-sets, and has prepared these studies in a way that will capture their attention and lead to greater maturity in Christ. I heartily recommend these studies.

Rick Warren, Senior Pastor, Saddleback Valley Community Church

YOUTHBUILDERS GROUP BIBLE STUDIES

It's Relational—Students learn best when they talk—not when you talk. There is always a get acquainted section in the Warm Up. All the experiences are based on building community in your group.

It's Biblical—With no apologies, this series in unashamedly Christian. Every session has a practical, relevant Bible study.

It's Experiential—Studies show that young people retain up to 85 percent of the material when they are *involved* in action-oriented, experiential learning. The sessions use role-plays, discussion starters, case studies, graphs and other experiential, educational methods. *We believe it's a sin to bore a young person with the gospel.*

It's Interactive—This study is geared to get students feeling comfortable with sharing ideas and interacting with peers and leaders.

It's Easy to Follow—The sessions have been prepared by Jim Burns to allow the leader to pick up the material and use it. There is little preparation time on your part. Jim did the work for you.

It's Adaptable—You can pick and choose from several topics or go straight through the material as a whole study.

It's Age Appropriate—In the "Team Effort" section, one group experience relates best to junior high students while the other works better with high school students. Look at both to determine which option is best for your group.

It's Parent Oriented—The Parent Page helps you to do youth ministry at its finest. Christian education should take place in the home as well as in the church. The Parent Page is your chance to come alongside the parents and help them have a good discussion with their kids.

It's Proven—This material was not written by someone in an ivory tower. It was written for young people and has already been used with them. They love it.

HOW TO USE THIS STUDY

The 12 sessions are divided into three stand-alone units. Each unit has four sessions. You may choose to teach all 12 sessions consecutively. Or you may use only one unit. Or you may present individual sessions. You know your group best so you choose.

Each of the 12 sessions is divided into five sections.

Warm Up—Young people will stay in your youth group if they feel comfortable and make friends in the group. This section is designed for you and the students to get to know each other better. These activities are filled with history-giving and affirming questions and experiences.

Team Effort—Following the model of Jesus, the Master Teacher, these activities engage young people in the session. Stories, group situations, surveys and more bring the session to the students. There is an option for junior high/middle school students and one for high school students.

In the Word—Most young people are biblically illiterate. These Bible studies present the Word of God and encourage students to see the relevance of the Scriptures to their lives.

Things to Think About—Young people need the opportunity to really think through the issues at hand. These discussion starters get students talking about the subject and interacting on important issues.

Parent Page—A youth worker can only do so much. Reproduce this page and get it into the hands of parents. This tool allows quality parent/teen communication that really brings the session home.

THE BIBLE *TUCK-IN*™

It's a tear-out sheet you fold and place in your Bible, containing the essentials you'll need for teaching your group.

HERE'S HOW TO USE IT:

To prepare for the session, first study the session. Tear out the Bible *Tuck-In*™ and personalize it by making notes. Fold the Bible *Tuck-In*™ in half on the dotted line. Slip it into your Bible for easy reference throughout the session. The Key Verse, Biblical Basis and Big Idea at the beginning of the Bible *Tuck-In*™ will help you keep the session on track. With the Bible *Tuck-In*™ your students will see that your teaching comes from the Bible and won't be distracted by a leader's guide.

Unit I

HOW TO HELP
A FRIEND IN CRISIS

LEADER'S PEP TALK

Perhaps the greatest "discovery" in recent youth ministry history is the incredible effectiveness of peer ministry and peer counseling. Previously, these terms were more widely accepted within the secular community than among Christian educators. However, today we know that frequently the most effective ministry is accomplished peer to peer or friend to friend.

I vividly remember a winter camp where we had one of the finest youth speakers in the world speaking to our high school students. He did a great job presenting the gospel of Jesus Christ to our kids. My youth staff just kept coming up to me saying "this is some of the finest speaking we've ever heard." Sunday morning, before the main session, we offered seminars taught by the kids themselves. Lisa taught a session on self-image. I attended her seminar. To be honest it wasn't a polished presentation. Lisa did have a ton of Scriptures. She shared some personal struggles. Still the body and content of her material was really weak. That evening after the retreat I read the evaluations and was absolutely shocked to see that even though the kids did like our big-time speaker they rated Lisa's seminar even higher. Why? Student after student remarked that they could really relate to what Lisa was going through in her own life and faith journey. Peer ministry wins again!

One of your most important jobs as a youth worker is to cultivate peer ministry. If you can teach your students how to minister and counsel their friends, then you have gone a long way toward developing a lifestyle of servanthood in their lives. Our job is to create doers of the Word and not just hearers. I hope in this section you inspire your kids to be people helpers in the same manner as Jesus helped His friends minister to the people of Palestine.

I'm sure you've heard the statement "give a person a fish and feed him or her for a day, teach a person to fish and feed him or her for a lifetime." In a sense that's what this first section is about. You have the opportunity to give your students some lifelong skills and inspire them to be more effective people helpers with the skills of counseling, problem solving, active listening and a better understanding of two of life's most critical issues—death and dying.

These sessions have been tested with junior high and senior high students and hopefully will be a lot of fun. However, anytime you bring up crisis situations, you've got to be prepared for horror stories as well. Statistics tell us no matter what your group's size, denomination or theological perspective, these crisis issues have affected or will affect your students. Thank you, my friend and fellow youth worker, for tackling the not-so-easy task of helping kids deal with the more difficult issues of life. You are making a difference, and I for one commend you for your courage. God bless you.

HOW TO HELP A FRIEND

KEY VERSE

"I can do everything through him who gives me strength." Philippians 4:13

BIBLICAL BASIS

Exodus 18:17,18;
Proverbs 3:5,6;
Ecclesiastes 4:9-12;
Romans 5:3-5;
Galatians 6:2;
Philippians 2:3-8; 4:13;
1 Thessalonians 5:14;
James 1:19

THE BIG IDEA

You have the skills and ability to help a friend in crisis.

AIMS OF THIS SESSION

During this session you will guide students to:
- Examine a variety of ways to help friends who are in crisis;
- Discover biblical principles for ministering to their peers;
- Implement an effective peer-to-peer ministry.

WARM UP

CRAZY QUIZ—
A literal test of students' knowledge.

TEAM EFFORT— JUNIOR HIGH/ MIDDLE SCHOOL

FIND A CRISIS—
Students discuss the crises teens face.

TEAM EFFORT— HIGH SCHOOL

EXPRESSING FEELINGS—
A listing of a variety of emotions students may feel.

IN THE WORD

DEVELOPING HELPING SKILLS—
A Bible study on practical ways students can help friends.

THINGS TO THINK ABOUT (OPTIONAL)

Questions to get students thinking and talking about handling crises.

PARENT PAGE

A tool to get the session into the home and allow parents and young people to discuss how to help friends in need.

LEADER'S DEVOTIONAL

"Two are better than one, because they have a good return for their work: If one falls down, his friend can help him up. But pity the man who falls and has no one to help him up! Also, if two lie down together, they will keep warm. But how can one keep warm alone? Though one may be overpowered, two can defend themselves. A cord of three strands is not quickly broken" (Ecclesiastes 4:9-12).

"Frank, what's going on? Why are you giving me all your favorite CDs, your stereo and baseball card collection? You love this stuff! Why are you giving it to me?"

"No reason, Steve. I just want you to have it."

"Frank..."

"Okay, I'll tell you why, but you have to promise not to tell anyone. I mean, if you're really my friend, you've got to swear you won't tell anyone what I'm going to tell you."

"Sure, Frank. You know I can keep a promise. We're buds, right? But why all the secrecy about you giving me your stuff?"

Steve doesn't realize what he's just promised Frank. He doesn't understand what Frank's about to do. Steve's never known anyone, let alone his best friend, who was on the verge of committing suicide. Steve doesn't have a clue how to help his best friend.

Friends helping friends. That's an important vital role you have as a youth worker. You are a coach, instructor, trainer and guide in teaching young people how to help friends. In crisis situations, your influence can play a critical, invisible role in saving the life of a teenager.

Take Steve for example. If Steve attended your youth ministry and he happened to hear a talk on "How to Help a Suicidal Friend," he'd be equipped to save Frank's life instead of being an accomplice to end it. Steve would know the clues and signals a suicidal friend gives out before he or she ends his or her life. He'd be suspicious about Frank's ongoing depression and why he's suddenly giving away his favorite things. He would know to value life more than a secret promise. He would know who to call and how to get help for Frank. Steve would know how to save his best friend's life.

Whether it's picking a designated driver, spotting signs of physical abuse, understanding drug and alcohol addiction or developing simple listening skills, teaching the students in your youth ministry how to help a friend can mean the difference between life and death. The Bible is filled with practical helping skills students can easily incorporate into their faith and friendships. Never underestimate the power of God in your life and the significant influence you play in helping your students help their friends. God has called us to receive His life and to give His life away. When you help students help their friends, you do just that. (Written by Joey O'Connor.)

"Sorrow is like a precious treasure, shown only to friends."— African proverb

HOW TO HELP A FRIEND

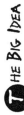K EY VERSE

"I can do everything through him who gives me strength." Philippians 4:13

B IBLICAL BASIS

Exodus 18:17,18; Proverbs 3:5,6; Ecclesiastes 4:9-12; Romans 5:3-5; Galatians 6:2; Philippians 2:3-8; 4:13; 1 Thessalonians 5:14; James 1:19

T HE BIG IDEA

You have the skills and ability to help a friend in crisis.

W ARM UP (10-15 MINUTES)
CRAZY QUIZ
• Give each student a copy of "Crazy Quiz" on pages 19 and 21 and a pen or pencil, or display the page using an overhead projector.

• Have students complete the page.

• Award a prize to any student who can answer all 20 questions correctly.
1. If you went to bed at 8 o'clock a.m. and set the alarm to get up at 9 o'clock the next morning, how many hours of sleep would you get? (One hour.)
2. Does England have a Fourth of July? (Yes.)
3. Why can't a man living in Winston-Salem, North Carolina, be buried west of the Mississippi River? (Because he's not dead.)
4. If you had a match and entered a room in which there were a kerosene lamp, an oil heater, and a wood-burning stove, which would you light first? (The match.)
5. Some months have 30 days, some have 31 days, how many months have 28 days? (They all do.)
6. A man builds a house with four sides to it, and it is rectangular in shape. Each side has a southern exposure. A big bear comes wandering by. What color is the bear? (White, it's a polar bear.)
7. How far can a dog run into the woods? (Halfway. The other half he's running out.)
8. What four words appear on every denomination of U.S. coin? ("United States of America" or "In God We Trust.")

Fold

Which helping skills do you need to work on most?

....

T HINGS TO THINK ABOUT (OPTIONAL)
• Use the questions on page 33 after or as a part of "In the Word."
1. A crisis is usually a matter of perception. Why do youth think some people "stress out" over getting pimples and others don't worry much even with traumatic experiences?

....

2. What keeps us from helping a friend in crisis?

....

3. What types of training do you wish you had to handle crises better?

....

P ARENT PAGE
• Distribute page to parents.

9. What is the minimum number of baseball players on the field during any part of an inning in a regular game? How many outs in an inning? (Ten—nine outfielders and a batter, six outs per inning.)
10. I have in my hand two U.S. coins which total 55 cents in value. One is not a nickel. What are the two coins? (A 50-cent piece and a nickel. One is not a nickel but the other is.)
11. A farmer had 17 sheep; all but nine died. How many does he have left? (Nine.)
12. Divide 30 by one-half and add 10. What is the answer? (Seventy.)
13. Take two apples from three apples and what do you have? (Two.)
14. An archeologist claimed he found some gold coins dated 46 B.C. Do you think he did? Explain. (No. A coin couldn't be dated B.C. [Before Christ] before Christ was born.)
15. A woman gives a beggar 50 cents. The woman is the beggar's sister but the beggar is not the woman's brother. How come? (They are sisters.)
16. How many animals of each species did Moses take aboard the Ark with him? (None. Noah took the animals, not Moses.)
17. Is it illegal in North Carolina for a man to marry his widow's sister? Why? (He is dead.)
18. What word in this test is misspelled? (Misspelled.)
19. From what animal do we get whale bones? (Whale.)
20. Where was Paul going on the road to Damascus? (Damascus.)

TEAM EFFORT—JUNIOR HIGH/MIDDLE SCHOOL (10-15 MINUTES)

FIND A CRISIS

- Divide students into groups of three or four.
- Ask each group to list as many crises as it can think of in three minutes.
- Allow each group to share its list of crises with the whole group.
- As a whole group develop a top-10 list of crises at school.

TEAM EFFORT—HIGH SCHOOL (10-15 MINUTES)

EXPRESSING FEELINGS

- Give each student a copy of "Expressing Feelings" on pages 23, 25, 27 and 29 and a pen or pencil, or display the page using an overhead projector.
- Have students complete the page.
- Allow students to share and discuss their answers with the whole group.

When helping friends in crisis, it's important to have them talk about their feelings and for you to get in touch with how they are feeling. Some people express feelings easily and others have real difficulty sharing their feelings. "The intensity of feelings" chart is a very helpful tool to use in identifying feelings and the intensity of the feelings. Read the chart and then write what someone might be feeling in each situation.

Feelings

___ My dad and mom are getting a divorce.
___ I've never told anyone, but I was sexually abused when I was 11 years old.
___ My best friend attempted suicide last night.

Fold

___ I had the best birthday ever.
___ I studied like crazy and my teacher only gave me a C on the exam.
___ I honestly could kill myself right now.
___ We went "all the way."
___ I drank a little too much at the party.
___ I feel far away from God.
___ I've been thinking about running away.
___ I'm embarrassed because of my weight.
___ I can't stop looking at those dirty videos.

IN THE WORD (25-30 MINUTES)

DEVELOPING HELPING SKILLS

- Give each student a copy of "Developing Helping Skills" on page 31 and a pen or pencil, or display the page using an overhead projector.
- As a whole group, complete the Bible study.
- As the leader, read through the "10 Principles for Helping Friends in Crisis" and comment where needed.

Read each Scripture below and determine the skills found in each passage that help people in crisis.

Scripture	Helping Skill
Exodus 18:17,18	(Not doing everything alone)
Proverbs 3:5,6	(Trust in God, faith)
Romans 5:3-5	(Perseverance, hopefulness)
Galatians 6:2	(Carry each other's burdens)
Philippians 2:3-8	(Servanthood, humility)
Philippians 4:13	(Finding strength in Christ)
1 Thessalonians 5:14	(Encourage, patience)
James 1:19	(Listening)

10 PRINCIPLES FOR HELPING FRIENDS IN CRISIS

1. Believe that God can use you to help others as He has helped you. Rely upon Him.
2. Silence is O.K.
3. If you feel you must speak, ask questions.
4. A major evaluation of our maturity is our ability to listen.
5. Remain calm and caring.
6. Don't have a judgmental spirit.
7. Confidentiality is vital.
8. Be prepared to seek additional help and support in referring a person to a professional.
9. Provide an optimistic relationship.
10. If you are helping a person solve a problem, remember that he or she must own the solution.

SO WHAT?

What helping skills come most easily for you?

WARM UP

CRAZY QUIZ[1]

1. If you went to bed at 8 o'clock a.m. and set the alarm to get up at 9 o'clock the next morning, how many hours of sleep would you get?

....

2. Does England have a Fourth of July?

....

3. Why can't a man living in Winston-Salem, North Carolina, be buried west of the Mississippi River?

....

4. If you had a match and entered a room in which there were a kerosene lamp, an oil heater, and a wood-burning stove, which would you light first?

....

5. Some months have 30 days, some have 31 days, how many months have 28 days?

....

6. A man builds a house with four sides to it, and it is rectangular in shape. Each side has a southern exposure. A big bear comes wandering by. What color is the bear?

....

7. How far can a dog run into the woods?

....

8. What four words appear on every denomination of U.S. coin?

....

9. What is the minimum number of baseball players on the field during any part of an inning in a regular game? How many outs in an inning?

....

10. I have in my hand two U.S. coins which total 55 cents in value. One is not a nickel. What are the two coins?

....

11. A farmer had 17 sheep; all but nine died. How many does he have left?

....

12. Divide 30 by one-half and add 10. What is the answer?

....

13. Take two apples from three apples and what do you have?

....

14. An archeologist claimed he found some gold coins dated 46 B.C. Do you think he did? Explain.

....

WARM UP

15. A woman gives a beggar 50 cents. The woman is the beggar's sister but the beggar is not the woman's brother. How come?

....

16. How many animals of each species did Moses take aboard the Ark with him?

....

17. Is it illegal in North Carolina for a man to marry his widow's sister? Why?

....

18. What word in this test is mispelled?

....

19. From what animal do we get whale bones?

....

20. Where was Paul going on the road to Damascus?

....

Note

1. *Ideas Numbers 13-16* (El Cajon, Calif: Youth Specialties, 1981), p. 11. Used by permission.

EAM EFFORT

EXPRESSING FEELINGS

When helping friends in crisis, it's important to have them talk about their feelings and for you to get in touch with how they are feeling. Some people express feelings easily and others have real difficulty sharing their feelings. "The Intensity of Feelings" chart is a very helpful tool to use in identifying feelings and the intensity of the feelings.

Read the chart and then write what someone might be feeling in each situation.

Feelings

.... My dad and mom are getting a divorce.

.... I've never told anyone, but I was sexually abused when I was 11 years old.

.... My best friend attempted suicide last night.

.... I had the best birthday ever.

.... I studied like crazy and my teacher only gave me a C on the exam.

.... I honestly could kill myself right now.

.... We went "all the way."

.... I drank a little too much at the party.

.... I feel far away from God.

.... I've been thinking about running away.

.... I'm embarrassed because of my weight.

.... I can't stop looking at those dirty videos.

THE INTENSITY OF FEELINGS

STRONG

Happy	Caring	Depressed	Inadequate	Fearful
thrilled	tenderness	desolate	worthless	terrified
on cloud nine	toward	dejected	good for	frightened
ecstatic	affection for	hopeless	nothing	intimidated
overjoyed	captivated by	alienated	powerless	horrified
excited	attached to	depressed	helpless	desperate
elated	devoted to	gloomy	impotent	panicky
sensational	adoration	dismal	crippled	terror
exhilarated	loving	bleak	inferior	stricken
fantastic	infatuated	in despair	emasculated	stage fright
terrific	enamored	empty	useless	dread
on top of the	cherished	barren	finished	vulnerable
world	idolize	grieved	like a failure	paralyzed
turned on	worship	grief	washed-up	
euphoric		despair		
enthusiastic		grim		
delighted				
marvelous				
great				

Confused	Hurt	Angry	Lonely	Guilt/Shame
bewildered	crushed	furious	isolated	sick at heart
puzzled	destroyed	enraged	abandoned	unforgivable
baffled	ruined	seething	all alone	humiliated
perplexed	degraded	outraged	forsaken	disgraced
trapped	pain(ed)	infuriated	cut off	degraded
confounded	wounded	burned up		horrible
in a dilemma	devasted	hateful		mortified
befuddled	tortured	fighting mad		exposed
in a quandry	disgraced	nauseated		
full of	humiliated	violent		
questions	anguished	indignant		
confused	at the mercy of	hatred		
	cast off	galled		
	forsaken	vengeful		
	rejected			
	discarded			

MODERATE

Happy
cheerful
lighthearted
happy
serene
wonderful
up
aglow
glowing
in high
   spirits
jovial
riding high
elevated
neat

Caring
caring
fond of
regard
respectful
admiration
concern for
hold dear
prize
taken with
turned on
trust
close

Depressed
distressed
upset
downcast
sorrowful
demoralized
discouraged
miserable
pessimistic
tearful
weepy
rotten
awful
horrible
terrible
blue
lost
melancholy

Inadequate
inadequate
whipped
defeated
incompetent
inept
overwhelmed
ineffective
lacking
deficient
unable
incapable
small
insignificant
no good
immobilized
unfit
unimportant
incomplete

Fearful
afraid
scared
fearful
apprehensive
jumpy
shaky
threatened
distrustful
risky
alarmed
butterflies
awkward
defensive

Confused
mixed-up
disorganized
foggy
troubled
adrift
lost
at loose ends
going around
   in circles
disconcerted
frustrated
flustered
in a bind
ambivalent
disturbed
helpless
emboiled

Hurt
hurt
belittled
shot down
overlooked
abused
depreciated
criticized
defamed
censured
discredited
disparaged
laughed at
maligned
mistreated
ridiculed
devalued
scorned
mocked
scoffed at
used
exploited
debased
slammed
slandered
impugned
cheapened

Angry
resentful
irritated
hostile
annoyed
upset with
agitated
mad
aggravated
offended
antagonistic
exasperated
belligerent
mean
vexed
spiteful
vindictive

Lonely
lonely
alienated
estranged
remote
alone
apart from
   others
insulated from
   others

Guilt/Shame
ashamed
guilty
remorseful
crummy
to blame
lost face
demeaned

MILD

Happy	Caring	Depressed	Inadequate	Fearful
glad	warm	unhappy	lacking	nervous
good	toward	down	confidence	anxious
contented	friendly	low	unsure of	unsure
satisfied	like	bad	yourself	hesitant
gratified	positive	blah	uncertain	timid
pleasant	toward	disappointed	weak	shy
pleased		sad	inefficient	worried
fine		glum		uneasy
				bashful

Confused	Hurt	Angry	Lonely	Guilt/Shame
uncertain	put down	uptight	left out	regretful
unsure	neglected	disgusted	excluded	wrong
bothered	overlooked	bugged	lonesome	embarrassed
uncomfortable	minimized	turned off	distant	at fault
undecided	let down	put out	aloof	in error
	unappreciated	miffed		responsible for
	taken for	irked		blew it
	granted	perturbed		
		ticked off		

 N THE WORD

DEVELOPING HELPING SKILLS

Read each Scripture below and determine the skills found in each passage that help people in crisis.

Scripture	Helping Skill
Exodus 18:17,18	....
Proverbs 3:5,6	....
Romans 5:3-5	....
Galatians 6:2	....
Philippians 2:3-8	....
Philippians 4:13	....
1 Thessalonians 5:14	....
James 1:19	....

10 PRINCIPLES FOR HELPING FRIENDS IN CRISIS[1]

1. Believe that God can use you to help others as He has helped you. Rely upon Him.
2. Silence is O.K.
3. If you feel you must speak, ask questions.
4. A major evaluation of our maturity is our ability to listen.
5. Remain calm and caring.
6. Don't have a judgmental spirit.
7. Confidentiality is vital.
8. Be prepared to seek additional help and support in referring a person to a professional.
9. Provide an optimistic relationship.
10. If you are helping a person solve a problem, remember that he or she must own the solution.

SO WHAT?

What helping skills come most easily for you?

....

....

....

Which helping skills do you need to work on most?

....

....

....

Note

1. These principles are taken from the National Institute of Youth Ministry's Peer Leadership Training for student leaders. The material was developed by Chris Cannon. For more information on a Peer Leadership training event in your area, contact NIYM at (800) 397-9725.

*T*HINGS TO *T*HINK *A*BOUT

1. A crisis is usually a matter of perception. Why do youth think some people "stress out" over getting pimples and others don't worry much even with traumatic experiences?

....

....

....

2. What keeps us from helping a friend in crisis?

....

....

....

3. What types of training do you wish you had to handle crises better?

....

....

....

PARENT PAGE

DOIN' THE WORD

"But be doers of the word, and not hearers only" (James 1:22, *NKJV*).

Here's a chance as a family to help someone in crisis.

First: Identify at least one person or family you know who is in a crisis situation.

Next: Develop a plan to help the person or family and decide when you will help.

What:...

....

When:...

....

Where:...

....

How:...

....

Next: Pray about it. Take the problem and your plan to God. Go ahead and spend a few minutes praying together.

Last: Go do it!

Session 1 "How to Help a Friend"

Date...

COUNSELING: PEER MINISTRY

KEY VERSE

"Where there is no guidance, the people fall, but in abundance of counselors there is victory." Proverbs 11:14 (*NASB*)

BIBLICAL BASIS

Psalm 119:24;
Proverbs 11:14;
Matthew 28:18-20;
John 14:16,17; 15:12-17;
Romans 8:29; 12:8; 15:14;
Galatians 6:12;
Ephesians 4:15;
Colossians 3:16;
1 Thessalonians 2:8; 5:14,21;
2 Timothy 3:16,17;
James 5:16

THE BIG IDEA

Peer-to-peer ministry is often the most effective kind of ministry, and when students develop ministry skills, they have a lifelong ability to serve God.

AIMS OF THIS SESSION

During this session you will guide students to:
• Examine how to be peer-to-peer counselors;
• Discover skills and abilities for being effective lay ministers;
• Implement biblical decisions to minister to their peers.

WARM UP

MAY I HAVE YOUR AUTOGRAPH?—
Students search for the right people.

TEAM EFFORT— JUNIOR HIGH/ MIDDLE SCHOOL

WHAT KIND OF PERSONALITY DO YOU HAVE?—
A personality questionnaire.

TEAM EFFORT— HIGH SCHOOL

PROBLEM SOLVING—
The steps to effective problem resolution.

IN THE WORD

THIRTEEN DISTINCTIONS OF EFFECTIVE PEER COUNSELING BASED ON THE BIBLE AND RESEARCH—
A Bible study on how to help others.

THINGS TO THINK ABOUT (OPTIONAL)

Questions to get students thinking and talking about ministry to friends.

PARENT PAGE

A tool to get the session into the home and allow parents and young people to discuss friends.

LEADER'S DEVOTIONAL

"Your statutes are my delight; they are my counselors" (Psalm 119:24).

As Stephanie and Denise drove home after spending three hours in a local coffee shop catching up on one another's lives, Stephanie turned to Denise and said, "Denise, there's one more thing I need to tell you. It's been tearing me up all night and you're the only one I can trust with this."

"Go ahead, Stephanie. You can tell me anything."

"Remember the guy, John, I told you about tonight? Well, after a couple months of dating, we began sleeping together and just last week I found out I was pregnant. I couldn't believe it. I was so scared. My parents would kill me if they found out. So last Friday, I went to the clinic and had an abortion."

As Denise listened, Stephanie crumpled into her arms in tears. Stephanie went on to explain her intense feelings of guilt, confusion, sorrow and anger over the whole situation. Denise's care and compassion made Stephanie feel safe in the midst of her pain. This wasn't the first time Denise had a friend trust her with such sensitive information. Everyone knows they can trust Denise.

Does your youth ministry have a "Denise"? Though Denise isn't a trained professional counselor, she is respected by her peers as one who listens and understands. She is known for her Christlike compassion and empathy for people in pain. Denise is a peer counselor who has brought healing to many of her friends' lives.

I sincerely believe that teenagers can be extremely helpful and gifted counselors. One of the unfortunate myths of counseling is that professional counselors are the only ones equipped to help others. Through seeing many "Denises" in action, I've thankfully witnessed this myth debunked many times.

Encouraging your students to be counselors and ministers to their friends is an incredible way to unleash the power of Jesus Christ on their campuses. When you teach biblical ministry skills to students, you equip them for lifetimes of significant Kingdom work. One of the most critical measuring sticks of a healthy youth ministry is not how the adults minister to students, but how the students minister to one another. Just as Jesus modeled peer ministry to His disciples, you are an ambassador of Christ of the importance of peer ministry to your students. (Written by Joey O'Connor.)

"A man is never what he is in spite of his circumstances, but because of them."—Oswald Chambers

COUNSELING: PEER MINISTRY

KEY VERSE

"Where there is no guidance, the people fall, but in abundance of counselors there is victory."
Proverbs 11:14 (NASB)

BIBLICAL BASIS

Psalm 119:24; Proverbs 11:14; Matthew 28:18-20; John 14:16,17; 15:12-17; Romans 8:29; 12:8; 15:14; Galatians 6:12; Ephesians 4:15; Colossians 3:16; 1 Thessalonians 2:8; 5:14,21; 2 Timothy 3:16,17; James 5:16

THE BIG IDEA

Peer-to-peer ministry is often the most effective kind of ministry, and when students develop ministry skills, they have a lifelong ability to serve God.

WARM UP (5-10 MINUTES)
MAY I HAVE YOUR AUTOGRAPH?

• Give each student a copy of "May I Have Your Autograph?" on page 41 and a pen or pencil.
• Have students complete the page.
• Give the winner a prize.
The object of this game is to be the first person to get all 10 autographs.
1. Find a person to sing "Twinkle, Twinkle Little Star."
2. Get autographs from three people of the opposite sex.
3. Ask someone to do 15 jumping jacks and have another person count them off aloud.
4. Find someone who is in love.
5. Find someone who is not in love but would like to be.
6. Play "Ring Around the Rosey" with someone. Sing aloud.
7. Find a person who likes cartoons. Have that person imitate his or her favorite character.
8. Ask someone to quote a Bible verse at the top of his or her lungs.

----- Fold -----

What core values for peer-to-peer ministry can you find in this Scripture?

What can we learn from Jesus' life concerning a biblical perspective on peer ministry?

Peer Counseling
"Where there is no guidance, the people fall, but in abundance of counselors there is victory" (Proverbs 11:14, NASB).

What is God's promise from this Scripture about a nation surrounding itself with wise counsel?

So What?
How can you apply these principles this week in your own life?

THINGS TO THINK ABOUT (OPTIONAL)

• Use the questions on page 55 after or as a part of "In the Word."

1. Many people believe that teen-to-teen ministry is more effective than adult-to-teen ministry. Do you agree?

2. Why is it sometimes difficult to counsel a friend effectively?

3. How could developing a ministry to your friends benefit you?

PARENT PAGE

• Distribute page to parents.

TEAM EFFORT—JUNIOR HIGH/MIDDLE SCHOOL (15-20 MINUTES)

WHAT KIND OF PERSONALITY DO YOU HAVE?

- Give each student a copy of "What Kind of Personality Do You Have?" on pages 43, 45 and 47 and a pen or pencil, or display the page using an overhead projector.
- Have students complete the page.

TEAM EFFORT—HIGH SCHOOL (15-20 MINUTES)

PROBLEM SOLVING

- Give each student a copy of "Problem Solving" on page 49 or display the page using an overhead projector.
- Explain the formula for getting to a problem and solving it thoroughly.
- Ask students to share a crisis or problem. Then work through the formula.
- Make sure students:

List at least three alternative solutions.

Select a specific plan of action.

Establish the accountability needed.

Set up the evaluation procedure.

Another aspect of helping a friend in crisis is problem solving. Here's a simple yet profound "formula" for getting to the real problem and solving it thoroughly:

Find the Real Problem.

List Alternative Solutions.

Select a Plan of Action.

Establish and Enforce Accountability.

Set Up an Evaluation Procedure.

1. **Find the real problem.**
If we jump into problem solving too quickly in the discussion, we may miss the real problem. It is important to be direct and ask what your friend considers the problem to be. Sometimes you'll need to ask "what's on your mind?" or else your friend may never get to the point.

2. **List alternative solutions.**
Once you have assisted in clarifying the problem, you can help your friend look at various alternatives to the solution. Consider the consequences of each alternative.

3. **Select a plan of action.**
If one of the alternatives seems to be the best idea, then work on the problem by using that plan. Sometimes it's very helpful to role-play or rehearse the plan.

4. **Establish and enforce accountability.**
Most action plans will not be as beneficial as they could be unless there's some method of accountability. Develop an easy plan of accountability.

5. **Set up an evaluation procedure.**
As part of the problem-solving accountability plan, develop some method of evaluation. We all need to see small chunks of success along the way. Don't look for perfection, but rather find a method that will encourage attainment of your friend's goals.

IN THE WORD (25-30 MINUTES)

THIRTEEN DISTINCTIONS OF EFFECTIVE PEER COUNSELING BASED ON THE BIBLE AND RESEARCH

- Give each student a copy of "Thirteen Distinctions of Effective Peer Counseling" on pages 51 and 53 and a pen or pencil.
- As a whole group, complete the Bible study.
  - The Holy Spirit's ministry as Counselor or Comforter is crucial (see John 14:16,17). Depend on Him in prayer for guidance, wisdom and healing power.
  - The Bible is a basic guide to helping people with problems (see 2 Timothy 3:16,17). Use it wisely and appropriately when possible.
  - Prayer is a crucial part of effective biblical peer counseling (see James 5:16). Pray with and for the counselee when possible.
  - The ultimate goal of peer counseling is to help Christians become more like Jesus (see Romans 8:29), or to grow spiritually, and to help non-Christians come closer to knowing Jesus as their own Lord and Savior, and therefore fulfill the Great Commission (see Matthew 28:18-20).
  - The personal spiritual qualities of the peer counselor are important: especially goodness or love, knowledge of the Bible (see Romans 15:14), wisdom (see Colossians 3:16), maturity (see Galatians 6:1,2), and the spiritual gift of exhortation or encouragement (see Romans 12:8).
  - The counselee's attitude, motivations and desire for help are crucial. Those who are actively involved in their counseling do better than those who are withdrawn, defensive or hostile.
  - The quality of the relationship between the peer counselor and the counselee is very important. There should be good rapport and communication based on empathy (understanding), respect (caring), concreteness (being specific), genuineness (being real), confrontation (telling it like it is), and immediacy (what's really going on between the two of you). The Bible calls this "speaking the truth in love" (Ephesians 4:15).
  - Effective peer counseling involves exploration, understanding and action phases, with a focus on changing problem thinking. Active listening and problem-solving skills are crucial.
  - The style of approach in peer counseling should be flexible depending on the counselee and the problem (see 1 Thessalonians 5:14).
  - The specific techniques or methods of counseling should be consistent with the Bible's teaching and values (see 1 Thessalonians 5:21).
  - Cultural sensitivity and cross-cultural counseling skills are needed by the peer counselor.
  - Skills in outreach and prevention are also important—for example, helping counselees to be connected to appropriate resources or community help and social support, including church and parachurch youth groups.
  - Awareness of their own limitations and knowing when and how to refer are also important for Christian peer counselors.

A Look at Biblical Perspective of Peer Ministry and Counseling

Peer Ministry

"My command is this: Love each other as I have loved you. Greater love has no one than this, that he lay down his life for his friends. You are my friends if you do what I command. I no longer call you servants, because a servant does not know his master's business. Instead, I have called you friends, for everything that I learned from my Father I have made known to you: You did not choose me, but I chose you and appointed you to go and bear fruit—fruit that will last. Then the Father will give you whatever you ask in my name. This is my command: Love each other" (John 15:12-17).

 ARM UP

MAY I HAVE YOUR AUTOGRAPH?

The object of this game is to be the first person to get all 10 autographs.

1. Find a person to sing "Twinkle, Twinkle Little Star."

....

2. Get autographs from three people of the opposite sex.

....

....

....

3. Ask someone to do 15 jumping jacks and have another person count them off aloud.

....

4. Find someone who is in love.

....

5. Find someone who is not in love but would like to be.

....

6. Play "Ring Around the Rosey" with someone. Sing aloud.

....

7. Find a person who likes cartoons. Have that person imitate his or her favorite character.

....

8. Ask someone to quote a Bible verse at the top of his or her lungs.

....

TEAM EFFORT

WHAT KIND OF PERSONALITY DO YOU HAVE?[1]

Every person is a unique instrument created by God. However, we tend to develop along the lines of similar personalities. It's important to know your personality style in order to be a student leader and a peer counselor. Here is a fun way to find out what kind of a personality you tend to have. This will also help you as you help others if you can understand a little of their personality structures.

1. I like to
a. think fast and take charge of a situation.
b. think about complex things that most other people haven't even thought of.
c. listen to other people's problems and help create a solution.
d. have other people need me.

2. I like it best when someone shows me that he or she loves me by
a. surprising me with something.
b. letting me be myself.
c. hanging out with me, talking, telling me how he or she feels.
d. doing things I've asked for.

3. I like to give a friend
a. excitement and variety.
b. a chance to be independent.
c. love and compassion.
d. security.

4. I like to
a. do things on the spur of the moment.
b. give people intelligent information.
c. keep everybody happy and make everybody feel included.
d. be someone you can depend on.

5. You can count on me to
a. have "guts." I'm unafraid and strong.
b. be smart.
c. be understanding.
d. be responsible.

6. I'm always looking for
a. excitement.
b. explanations.
c. peace.
d. order.

7. The people who know me best would probably say I'm
a. competitive and ready to go for it.
b. quiet and organized.
c. emotional and sensitive to other people's feelings.
d. loyal; I follow the rules.

8. I have this drive to be
a. free and allowed to do things spontaneously.
b. logical and on top of things.
c. accepted by other people.
d. in control of my little world.

9. When I'm really down, I usually
a. lash out at people or act rude.
b. go off by myself or become really sarcastic.
c. cry or mope around.
d. feel sorry for myself.

10. When I'm hanging out with friends, I usually
a. have a blast and enjoy myself.
b. mostly talk to one or two people.
c. make sure everyone is having a good time and feels included.
d. take charge when it's time to order the pizza or gather the funds for a movie.

TEAM EFFORT

Scoring: Add up all the A's and write the total next to A below. Do the same for the B's, C's and D's. The column with the highest number of points is you! The descriptions below will tell you more about the personality that God has blessed you with.

___ A   ___ B   ___ C   ___ D

A: You love nothing more than simply having a good time! When it comes to trying something new, you possess energy you haven't even used yet—and that something "new" often involves performing in front of other people...or should we say showing off? (In a fun way, of course!) Talent? You have a lot of it. You get bored fast, though, and you hate chores and school activities that involve a lot of drills and routines. You really like to do what you want, when you want, which makes it hard for you to follow rules and respect authority just because it's there. Your room at home and your locker at school probably won't win any prizes for neatness. In the friendship category, you like people who are willing to try new things and you have no problem taking the lead. You're a touchy-feely person, but you also like competition. Your friends can count on your surprises of off-the-wall or extravagant things or your bizarre, spur-of-the-moment suggestions. You learn best by experience, and you like to figure things out for yourself. In a nutshell? Life is a banquet, and you aren't going to go hungry!

B: You don't fit anyone's mold! You're always curious about how and why things work. You love the abstract because you enjoy analyzing. When you're making a decision, it could take weeks! You're inventive, though, and if there's a new way to do something, you're the first one to try it...then modify it. You're very independent, and you don't show your emotions because you make decisions based on thoughts and facts, not feelings. You like having friends, and they know you love them, but you don't talk about it much. What for? They already know! You enjoy a challenge—especially in school—and you'll study for hours or weeks or weekends on a project as long as it's interesting to you. But drills and worksheets? Forget it! You don't automatically accept the rules; they have to make sense to you. Life is good for you because the possibilities are endless!

C: You love feelings! People often come to you with their problems because you love to talk about the way you feel and how they feel. You also have a great imagination! Since you hate conflict, you'd rather have a root canal than confront somebody. But you love helping people get out of a bind and on the right track again. You're definitely a romantic, so you tend to make decisions based on how you feel rather than on what you think. You're convinced that true love is out there and that it's possible to live happily ever after. People are your life, and the people in your life get flowers, poems, cards and notes from you. You absolutely LOVE life, and you're always looking for its real meaning. You respond well to encouragement and approval, but you're not crazy about competition. You like things where everybody wins—there are no losers. You're deeply committed—to your friends, your family and God. If there's someone most everybody loves, it's you!

D: If people want something done, they come to you because you're like a rock. No matter how boring and detailed the schoolwork or job is, you stick to it until it's done. Even your P.E. locker is organized—not to mention your makeup case, your CD's and your underwear drawer! You respond to those in charge and have no problem following the rules. But you do have a problem when things get chaotic. You hate classes where the teacher has no control, or parties where people go wild. You're a serious person. How do you show people you love them? By doing things for them, like baking cookies for your boyfriend or doing the dishes for your mom when she's wiped out. You know what's right and wrong and you live your life accordingly. Big changes make you nervous, and you feel guilty when you mess up (though that doesn't happen very often!). Though no one's perfect, you're pretty close.

Team Effort

Remember, no single personality is better than another. God loves everyone He created. The important thing is for you to know and love who you are. Why? Because THEN you can strengthen your good points and work on your weak ones. It also helps to understand who other people are. It sure makes getting along a whole lot easier!

Note

1. Adapted from Nancy N. Rue, "What Kind of Personality Do You Have?" *Brio* 5, no. 10 (October, 1994): 25-26. Used by permission.

 **T**EAM EFFORT

PROBLEM SOLVING

Another aspect of helping a friend in crisis is problem solving. Here's a simple yet profound "formula" for getting to the real problem and solving it thoroughly:

Find the Real Problem.
  List Alternative Solutions.
    Select a Plan of Action.
      Establish and Enforce Accountability.
        Set Up an Evaluation Procedure.

1. Find the real problem.

   If we jump into problem solving too quickly in the discussion, we may miss the real problem. It is important to be direct and ask what your friend considers the problem to be. Sometimes you'll need to ask "what's on your mind?" or else your friend may never get to the point.

2. List alternative solutions.

   Once you have assisted in clarifying the problem, you can help your friend look at various alternatives to the solution. Consider the consequences of each alternative.

3. Select a plan of action.

   If one of the alternatives seems to be the best idea, then work on the problem by using that plan. Sometimes it's very helpful to role-play or rehearse the plan.

4. Establish and enforce accountability.

   Most action plans will not be as beneficial as they could be unless there's some method of accountability. Develop an easy plan of accountability.

5. Set up an evaluation procedure.

   As part of the problem-solving accountability plan, develop some method of evaluation. We all need to see small chunks of success along the way. Don't look for perfection, but rather find a method that will encourage attainment of your friend's goals.

 **IN THE WORD**

**COUNSELING:
PEER MINISTRY**

THIRTEEN DISTINCTIONS OF EFFECTIVE PEER COUNSELING BASED ON THE BIBLE AND RESEARCH[1]

- The Holy Spirit's ministry as Counselor or Comforter is crucial (see John 14:16,17). Depend on Him in prayer for guidance, wisdom and healing power.
- The Bible is a basic guide to helping people with problems (see 2 Timothy 3:16,17). Use it wisely and appropriately when possible.
- Prayer is a crucial part of effective biblical peer counseling (see James 5:16). Pray with and for the counselee when possible.
- The ultimate goal of peer counseling is to help Christians become more like Jesus (see Romans 8:29), or to grow spiritually, and to help non-Christians come closer to knowing Jesus as their own Lord and Savior, and therefore fulfill the Great Commission (see Matthew 28:18-20).
- The personal spiritual qualities of the peer counselor are important: especially goodness or love, knowledge of the Bible (see Romans 15:14), wisdom (see Colossians 3:16), maturity (see Galatians 6:12), and the spiritual gift of exhortation or encouragement (see Romans 12:8).
- The counselee's attitude, motivations and desire for help are crucial. Those who are actively involved in their counseling do better than those who are withdrawn, defensive or hostile.
- The quality of the relationship between the peer counselor and the counselee is very important. There should be good rapport and communication based on empathy (understanding), respect (caring), concreteness (being specific), genuineness (being real), confrontation (telling it like it is), and immediacy (what's really going on between the two of you). The Bible calls this "speaking the truth in love" (Ephesians 4:15).
- Effective peer counseling involves exploration, understanding and action phases, with a focus on changing problem thinking. Active listening and problem-solving skills are crucial.
- The style of approach in peer counseling should be flexible depending on the counselee and the problem (see 1 Thessalonians 5:14).
- The specific techniques or methods of counseling should be consistent with the Bible's teaching and values (see 1 Thessalonians 5:21).
- Cultural sensitivity and cross-cultural counseling skills are needed by the peer counselor.
- Skills in outreach and prevention are also important—for example, helping counselees to be connected to appropriate resources or community help and social support, including church and parachurch youth groups.
- Awareness of their own limitations and knowing when and how to refer are also important for Christian peer counselors.

A LOOK AT THE BIBLICAL PERSPECTIVE OF PEER MINISTRY AND COUNSELING

PEER MINISTRY

"My command is this: Love each other as I have loved you. Greater love has no one than this, that he lay down his life for his friends. You are my friends if you do what I command. I no longer call you servants, because a servant does not know his master's business. Instead, I have called you friends, for everything that I learned from my Father I have made known to you. You did not choose me, but I chose you and appointed you to go and bear fruit—fruit that will last. Then the Father will give you whatever you ask in my name. This is my command: Love each other" (John 15:12-17).

N THE WORD

What core values for peer-to-peer ministry can you find in this Scripture?

....

....

....

What can we learn from Jesus' life concerning a biblical perspective on peer ministry?

....

....

....

PEER COUNSELING

"Where there is no guidance, the people fall, but in abundance of counselors there is victory" (Proverbs 11:14, *NASB*).

What is God's promise from this Scripture about a nation surrounding itself with wise counsel?

....

....

....

SO WHAT?

How can you apply these principles this week in your own life?

....

....

....

....

Note

1. Adapted from Joan Sturkie, *Peer Counseling in Youth Groups* (Grand Rapids, Mich.: Zondervan Publishing, 1992), p. 92. Used by permission.

THINGS TO THINK ABOUT

1. Many people believe that teen-to-teen ministry is more effective than adult-to-teen ministry. Do you agree?

....

....

....

2. Why is it sometimes difficult to counsel a friend effectively?

....

....

....

3. How could developing a ministry to your friends benefit you?

....

....

....

PARENT PAGE

INFLUENTIAL PEOPLE

Parent Questions

Who were your best friends when you were growing up?

....

....

Who were some of your heroes when you were young?

....

....

If you had your life to live over again, what would you do differently?

....

....

Student Questions

Name five influential people in your life.

....

....

....

If you could have a peer ministry with a friend, who would it be with and what would you do?

....

....

Is there a peer that counsels you? If so, who?

....

....

"We loved you so much that we were delighted to share with you not only the gospel of God but our lives as well, because you had become so dear to us" (1 Thessalonians 2:8).

How would you describe Paul's philosophy of ministry from this Scripture?

....

....

How could you minister to each other more effectively?

....

....

Session 2 "Counseling: Peer Ministry"

Date..

LISTENING: THE LANGUAGE OF LOVE

K EY VERSE

"He who answers before listening—
that is his folly and his shame."
Proverbs 18:13

B IBLICAL BASIS

Psalm 116:1,2;
Proverbs 18:13;
John 4:4-26

T HE BIG IDEA

Listening is the language of love. One
of the greatest ministries you can have
is to be an active listener.

A IMS OF THIS SESSION

During this session you will guide students to:
• Examine the ministry tool of active
  listening;
• Discover new skills of active listening;
• Implement a higher degree of ability
  to counsel and listen.

W ARM UP

COMMUNICATION BREAKDOWN—

A game showing bad communication.

T EAM EFFORT— JUNIOR HIGH/ MIDDLE SCHOOL

FRIEND TO FRIEND—

Students practice communicating
one-on-one.

T EAM EFFORT— HIGH SCHOOL

ACTIVE LISTENING ROLE-PLAY—

Students practice listening and being
heard.

I N THE WORD

JESUS AND THE WOMAN AT THE WELL—

A Bible study on Jesus' model of
listening.

T HINGS TO THINK ABOUT (OPTIONAL)

Questions to get students thinking
and talking about good listening.

P ARENT PAGE

A tool to get the session into the
home and allow parents and
young people to discuss listening
to each other.

LEADER'S DEVOTIONAL

"I love the Lord, for he heard my voice; he heard my cry for mercy. Because he turned his ear to me, I will call on him as long as I live" (Psalm 116:1,2).

Tennessee. Arkansas. Oklahoma. Texas. New Mexico. Arizona. And finally California. After twenty-nine hundred miles, Mike and I finally crossed the border into California. Two-and-a-half days of driving west—two-and-a-half days of listening. What began as a series of phone calls from Mike in Tennessee eventually led me to catch a late-night, red-eye flight to Nashville.

A former student in our high school and college ministry, Mike joined the Army Reserves and moved to Nashville a year earlier. He met a girl and after only a couple of months of dating, they quickly got engaged. Two months later, the engagement was off and the relationship over.

Mike was in trouble. Depressed. Possibly suicidal. He was drinking a lot, and worse, he was all alone. Alone with his thoughts. Alone with his pain.

When I arrived in Nashville, Mike wasn't proud of himself or his actions. He felt extremely guilty for serious mistakes he made with his former fiancée. Never had he been so far from God or himself. Mike's life was a mess and nobody knew it better than he.

Mike didn't need a sermon, a few choice Scriptures or helpful advice from me. All he needed was for me to listen. So that's what I did. Two-and-a-half days of driving and listening.

Whether you've been serving young people for years or this is your very first week planning a youth Bible study, one of the most precious, valuable gifts you can give your students is the gift of listening. Listening is the language of love and when you listen to the thoughts, struggles and needs of teenagers, you are the ears of Christ to them.

Students won't be impressed by your biblical knowledge or life experiences if they don't sense you really care. Listening is a simple, specific way to show your love to them. Listening is one of the most practical ways to demonstrate the love of God. Actively listening to students, whether they are in a serious crisis like Mike or if they just want a simple answer to a simple question, is an authentic demonstration of Jesus Christ. Young people will be more inclined to listen to God if you first listen to them. (Written by Joey O'Connor.)

"No matter how good the communication, if no one listens all is lost. The best communication forces you to listen."—Max DePree

LISTENING: THE LANGUAGE OF LOVE

K EY VERSE

"He who answers before listening—that is his folly and his shame." Proverbs 18:13

B IBLICAL BASIS

Psalm 116:1,2; Proverbs 18:13; John 4:4-26

T HE BIG IDEA

Listening is the language of love. One of the greatest ministries you can have is to be an active listener.

W ARM UP (10-15 MINUTES)

COMMUNICATION BREAKDOWN

• Ask four to six students to leave the room.
• Have two of the students return and have one of them tell the other student a 20- to 30-second story.
• Have each of the other students return one at a time to hear the story from the previous student. Student Two tells Student Three the story, Student Three tells Student Four, etc.
• Compare the original story told by Student One with the story told by the last student. Discuss the breakdown in communication.

T EAM EFFORT—JUNIOR HIGH/ MIDDLE SCHOOL (10-15 MINUTES)

FRIEND TO FRIEND

• Divide students into pairs.
• Explain the three questions of J. David Stone for good communication:
What is it you want?
How are you feeling?
What are you going to do?
• Instruct students to share a problem with their partners and then have the partners ask the three questions.
• Briefly discuss answers.

ACTIVE LISTENING ROLE-PLAY

- Invite two people to stand in front of your group.
- Ask one of the students to share a problem in less than three minutes.
- Have the other student tell what he or she heard.
- Invite the rest of the class to add anything else they heard the "counselee" share about the problem.
- Explain these four helpful listening questions. Then repeat the exercise with different students.
  1. What emotion is the person feeling?
  2. Are there any camouflaged feelings?
  3. Is the person talking about his or her root problem?
  4. How can I share empathy or caring with him or her?

IN THE WORD (25-30 MINUTES)

JESUS AND THE WOMAN AT THE WELL

- Give each student a copy of "Jesus and the Woman at the Well" on pages 63 and 65 and a pen or pencil, or display the page using an overhead projector.
- Read the account in John 4:4-26 aloud to the whole group.
- As a whole group, complete the Bible study.

Now try to listen to what the woman was really saying in each of her statements as Jesus did. After each of her statements, paraphrase in your own language what point or points she was really trying to communicate.

"You are a Jew and I am a Samaritan woman. How can you ask me for a drink?" (v. 9). What was she *really* saying?

"Sir," the woman said, "you have nothing to draw with and the well is deep. Where can you get this living water? Are you greater than our father Jacob, who gave us the well and drank from it himself, as did also his sons and his flocks and herds?" (vv. 11,12). What was she *really* saying?

"Sir, give me this water so that I won't get thirsty and have to keep coming here to draw water" (v. 15). What was she *really* saying?

"I have no husband" (v. 17). What was she *really* saying?

"Sir," the woman said, "I can see that you are a prophet. Our fathers worshiped on this mountain, but you Jews claim that the place where we must worship is in Jerusalem" (vv. 19,20). What was she *really* saying?

Fold

"I know that Messiah" (called Christ) "is coming. When he comes, he will explain everything to us" (v. 25). What was she *really* saying?

SO WHAT?

What are they *really* saying?

The "echo technique" or "reflection listening" is when someone shares a statement with you, and you then restate the point to see if you truly understand what he or she said.

Here's an example:

Counselee: "I hate math class, and my teacher is the worst."

Counselor: "It sounds like you are really frustrated with your math teacher and the class."

With one other person, practice the "echo technique." Role-play the part of the counselee twice and role-play the counselor twice.

THINGS TO THINK ABOUT (OPTIONAL)

- Use the questions on page 67 after or as a part of "In the Word."

1. What keeps most people from being good listeners?

2. Some people call listening "the language of love." Why?

3. Who is someone you know who is an excellent listener? What are the results of his or her ability to listen?

PARENT PAGE

- Distribute page to parents.

IN THE WORD

JESUS AND THE WOMAN AT THE WELL

"Now he had to go through Samaria. So he came to a town in Samaria called Sychar, near the plot of ground Jacob had given to his son Joseph. Jacob's well was there, and Jesus, tired as he was from the journey, sat down by the well. It was about the sixth hour.

"When a Samaritan woman came to draw water, Jesus said to her, 'Will you give me a drink?' (His disciples had gone into the town to buy food.)

"The Samaritan woman said to him, 'You are a Jew and I am a Samaritan woman. How can you ask me for a drink?' (For Jews do not associate with Samaritans.)

"Jesus answered her, 'If you knew the gift of God and who it is that asks you for a drink, you would have asked him and he would have given you living water.'

"'Sir,' the woman said, 'you have nothing to draw with and the well is deep. Where can you get this living water? Are you greater than our father Jacob, who gave us the well and drank from it himself, as did also his sons and his flocks and herds?'

"Jesus answered, 'Everyone who drinks this water will be thirsty again, but whoever drinks the water I give him will never thirst. Indeed, the water I give him will become in him a spring of water welling up to eternal life.'

"The woman said to him, 'Sir, give me this water so that I won't get thirsty and have to keep coming here to draw water.'

"He told her, 'Go, call your husband and come back.'

"'I have no husband,' she replied.

"Jesus said to her, 'You are right when you say you have no husband. The fact is, you have had five husbands, and the man you now have is not your husband. What you have just said is quite true.'

"'Sir,' the woman said, 'I can see that you are a prophet. Our fathers worshiped on this mountain, but you Jews claim that the place where we must worship is in Jerusalem.'

"Jesus declared, 'Believe me, woman, a time is coming when you will worship the Father neither on this mountain nor in Jerusalem. You Samaritans worship what you do not know; we worship what we do know, for salvation is from the Jews. Yet a time is coming and has now come when the true worshipers will worship the Father in spirit and truth, for they are the kind of worshipers the Father seeks. God is spirit, and his worshipers must worship in spirit and in truth.'

"The woman said, 'I know that Messiah' (called Christ) 'is coming. When he comes, he will explain everything to us.'

"Then Jesus declared, 'I who speak to you am he'" (John 4:4-26).

Now try to listen to what the woman was really saying in each of her statements as Jesus did. After each of her statements, paraphrase in your own language what point or points she was really trying to communicate.

"You are a Jew and I am a Samaritan woman. How can you ask me for a drink?" (v. 9). What was she *really* saying?

....

....

IN THE WORD

"'Sir,' the woman said, 'you have nothing to draw with and the well is deep. Where can you get this living water? Are you greater than our father Jacob, who gave us the well and drank from it himself, as did also his sons and his flocks and herds?'" (vv. 11,12). What was she *really* saying?

....

....

"Sir, give me this water so that I won't get thirsty and have to keep coming here to draw water" (v. 15). What was she *really* saying?

....

....

"I have no husband" (v. 17). What was she *really* saying?

....

....

"'Sir,' the woman said, 'I can see that you are a prophet. Our fathers worshiped on this mountain, but you Jews claim that the place where we must worship is in Jerusalem'" (vv. 19,20). What was she *really* saying?

....

....

"'I know that Messiah' (called Christ) 'is coming. When he comes, he will explain everything to us'" (v. 25). What was she *really* saying?

....

....

....

SO WHAT?

What are they *really* saying?

The "echo technique" or "reflection listening" is when someone shares a statement with you, and you then restate the point to see if you truly understand what he or she said.

Here's an example:

Counselee: "I hate math class, and my teacher is the worst."

Counselor: "It sounds like you are really frustrated with your math teacher and the class."

With one other person, practice the "echo technique." Role-play the part of the counselee twice and role-play the counselor twice.

THINGS TO **T**HINK **A**BOUT

1. What keeps most people from being good listeners?

....

....

....

2. Some people call listening "the language of love." Why?

....

....

....

3. Who is someone you know who is an excellent listener? What are the results of his or her ability to listen?

....

....

....

 **PARENT PAGE**

LISTENING: THE LANGUAGE OF LOVE

"He who answers before listening—that is his folly and his shame" (Proverbs 18:13).

Say this verse in your own words.

How could listening before answering help your family's communication?

....

....

....

When and about what do you need to have your family listen to you?

....

....

Take a few moments to talk and listen. The listeners are not allowed to interrupt or respond until after the talker is finished.
• Tell a fun story about something that happened to you this year.
• Share a burden.
• Share a blessing.

Session 3 "Listening: The Language of Love" Date ....

DEATH AND DYING

Key Verses

"Do not let your hearts be troubled. Trust in God; trust also in me. In my Father's house are many rooms; if it were not so, I would have told you. I am going there to prepare a place for you. And if I go and prepare a place for you, I will come back and take you to be with me that you also may be where I am."
John 14:1-3

Biblical Basis

Deuteronomy 31:8;
Psalms 23; 46; 118:24; 150:2,6;
John 3:16; 10:10; 14;
Romans 5:8; 6:4,5; 8;
Colossians 1:27;
2 Timothy 1:10;
1 John 2:25; 5:13

The Big Idea

The ultimate fact of life is that we will all die. Confronting the problems of death and dying from God's perspective will help us to better understand what death is and how we can live our lives to the fullest.

Aims of This Session

During this session you will guide students to:
- Examine the uncomfortable issue of death;
- Discover and identify the biblical principles associated with death and dying;
- Implement positive and hopeful views of life and death.

Warm Up

Your Family Tree—
Students chart their families.

Team Effort— Junior High/ Middle School

Your Gravestone—
A glimpse into what students would like their lives to be like.

Team Effort— High School

Grief—
Students work through the process of grief.

In the Word

On Death and Dying—
A Bible study on God's life in spite of death.

Things to Think About (optional)

Questions to get students thinking and talking about dealing with death.

Parent Page

A tool to get the session into the home and allow parents and young people to discuss the reality of death.

Leader's Devotional

"We were therefore buried with him through baptism into death in order that, just as Christ was raised from the dead through the glory of the Father, we too may live a new life. If we have been united with him like this in his death, we will certainly also be united with him in his resurrection" (Romans 6:4,5).

"Some of you sitting in this room tonight will not live to see your 20th birthday. Some of you will not graduate from college or ever get married. Look around the room—some of your closest friends may not be alive a few years from now."

So went my challenge about choosing between life or death to a living room packed with high school students. Death always seems to capture their attention. Though death is a topic most people want to quietly ignore, death is a subject to which young people are surprisingly open.

Perhaps the reason I'm not afraid to talk about death is because my father is a mortician. A slight advantage you could say, but nevertheless, students are willing to talk about death because it causes them to consider their decisions about life. Your willingness to talk about the reality of death to students can be the bridge God uses to lead them to life in Jesus Christ.

Death is a subject most parents, teachers and friends avoid talking about. You can be God's instrument to help students understand what the Bible says about death, how to handle grief, what to say to dying relatives and how to have hope in a world filled with death. You are in a unique position to challenge students to live life to the fullest.

Preparing this lesson on death and dying may prompt you to think about how death has affected you. Perhaps the simplest, most effective introduction to this sensitive subject is to share your personal experience of losing a loved one. Sharing how you dealt with feelings of grief, anger, sadness and loss can create a safe environment for students to share their feelings. Most of all, I hope this lesson encourages and motivates you to rejoice in the life you have in Jesus Christ. Jesus has overcome death, sadness and dying. You can rejoice and be thankful in His life, death and resurrection for you. (Written by Joey O'Connor.)

"No one ever told me that grief felt so like fear. I am not afraid, but the sensation is like being afraid. The same fluttering in the stomach, the same restlessness, the yawning. I keep on swallowing."—C. S. Lewis

DEATH AND DYING

KEY VERSES

"Do not let your hearts be troubled. Trust in God; trust also in me. In my Father's house are many rooms; if it were not so, I would have told you. I am going there to prepare a place for you. And if I go and prepare a place for you, I will come back and take you to be with me that you also may be where I am." John 14:1-3

BIBLICAL BASIS

Deuteronomy 31:8; Psalms 23; 46; 118:24; 150:2,6; John 3:16; 10:10; 14; Romans 5:8; 6:4,5; 8; Colossians 1:27; 2 Timothy 1:10; 1 John 2:25; 5:13

THE BIG IDEA

The ultimate fact of life is that we will all die. Confronting the problems of death and dying from God's perspective will help us to better understand what death is and how we can live our lives to the fullest.

WARM UP (10-15 MINUTES)

YOUR FAMILY TREE

• Give each student a copy of "Your Family Tree" on page 75 and a pen or pencil, or display the page using an overhead projector.
• Have students complete the page.
• As a whole group, discuss responses.
Fill in the chart and then the statements.

Grandma (Dad's mom)		Grandpa (Dad's dad)		Grandma (Mom's mom)		Grandpa (Mom's dad)
	Dad				Mom	
		Brothers and Sisters				
		Me				

The hospital or city I was born in is:

My most unique relative is:

---

6. Do not repress your fears about death and dying. Do you feel your fear of death and dying is normal? If you have never talked with someone about your fears do not be afraid to do so. There are no easy answers. However, there is someone near you with an understanding heart.

SO WHAT?

In the space provided below, write a prayer to God telling Him your greatest fears about death and dying. You may want to write about your fear of your own death or the death of a loved one. Write about your doubts of eternal life or about your thankfulness for the assurance of your salvation. After you have written about these feelings, talk with someone about your fears.

THINGS TO THINK ABOUT (OPTIONAL)

• Use the questions on page 85 after or as a part of "In the Word."

1. Why is it important to talk about our feelings concerning death?

2. How can our group encourage each other to be more honest with our feelings about death?

3. List some practical ways you could help when a special person in someone's life dies.

PARENT PAGE

• Distribute page to parents.

The family member who is most inspiring is: _____

TEAM EFFORT—JUNIOR HIGH/MIDDLE SCHOOL (10-15 Minutes)

YOUR GRAVESTONE

• Divide students into groups of three or four.

• Give each student a copy of "Your Gravestone" on page 77 and a pen or pencil, or display the page using an overhead projector.

• Have students complete the page.

The following may sound like a morbid activity but you will find it very meaningful. Write what you would like to have printed on your gravestone (even though the odds are you will live to be over 70 years of age). Sometimes when we think about what we want our lives to represent when we die, it is easier to set priorities to accomplish our desired goals.

Here's an example of what I would want to put on my gravestone: "Here is a man who walked in integrity. He was deeply committed to his family and friends and he was a positive influence for God's kingdom."

Now you try it.

TEAM EFFORT—HIGH SCHOOL (10-15 Minutes)

GRIEF

• Give each student a copy of "Grief" on page 79 and a pen or pencil, or display the page using an overhead projector.

• Have students complete the page.

• As a whole group, discuss the page.

Undoubtedly, if you haven't already, you will one day experience the excruciating pain and grief that come when a loved one dies.

grief (grēf), n. l. Grief may be called a life-shaking sorrow over loss. 2. Grief is a dark, heavy thing, and hard to penetrate. 3. The core of the grief experience is anxiety.

Here are a few points to remember about grief:

1. Grief is normal. You must grieve before you can go on with life. Never be afraid to cry or recognize your hurt. These feelings and emotions are normal.

2. Grief takes time. You will not get over your pain instantly. The dull ache will be with you for a long time.

3. Don't be afraid to talk about your hurt. As we talk and share our sorrows, we at times receive strength and mutual support.

4. There is comfort. Read Scriptures of peace, hope and victory over death. Here are a few to look up:

Psalm 23
Psalm 46
John 14
Romans 8

Fold

---

5. You can be a comfort to others. Read this beautiful illustration of comfort that Joseph Bayly writes about in his helpful book, *The View from a Hearse*. One of this children had died and this is how he received comfort:

"I was sitting, torn by grief. Someone came and talked to me of God's dealing, of why it happened, of hope beyond the grave. He talked constantly, he said things I knew were true. I was unmoved, except to wish he'd go away. He finally did.

"Another came and sat beside me. He didn't talk. He didn't ask leading questions. He just sat beside me for an hour and more, listened when I said something, answered briefly, prayed simply, left. I was moved. I was comforted. I hated to see him go."

IN THE WORD (25-30 Minutes)

ON DEATH AND DYING

• Give each student a copy of "On Death and Dying" on pages 81 and 83 and a pen or pencil, or display the page using an overhead projector.

• As a whole group, complete the Bible study.

1. Life is a gift. Since our very breath and lives are a gift from God, our attitudes should be that of thankfulness to God. Read the following verses and discuss how they relate to life being a gift to you from God:

Psalm 118:24 (God has given us each day of our lives.)

Psalm 150:2,6 (We should praise God for every breath, for being created by Him, for our lives, etc.)

Romans 5:8 (Even though we don't always live life the way God intended, He still loves us. He gave His Son, Jesus, for us.)

2. Life is eternal. Life on earth is but a snap of the fingers compared to eternity. As we go about living our lives, the element of eternal life is sometimes forgotten.

What does the Bible say about eternal life?

John 3:16 (If we believe in Jesus we will have eternal life.)

1 John 2:25 (We have been promised eternal life through Jesus.)

1 John 5:13 (If you believe in the name of Jesus, the Son of God, you may have eternal life.)

After reading these Scriptures, what are your hopes, dream, fears, doubts and joys? Write your feelings in the space below and then share with your group.

3. There is hope! God brings hope to those with a fear of death.

Read John 14:1-3.

What words of reassurance and comfort does Jesus give His followers? (Don't let your hearts be troubled. Trust in God and Jesus. Jesus is going to prepare a place for us. He will come back and take us to be with Him. We will be with Jesus always.)

According to 2 Timothy 1:10 what is the good news of the gospel? (Jesus has destroyed death. He has brought life and immortality to us through the gospel.)

What is your "hope of glory" according to Colossians 1:27? (Christ in you.)

4. God walks with you. Read Psalm 23.

How can this psalm be a comfort to those who fear death? (God promises to always be with us. He will be there to comfort us and walk with us whatever the circumstance.)

Find at least two principles in this great psalm that will help remind you that God is with you. (Students answer.)

Why is Deuteronomy 31:8 an important verse to plant in our hearts? (Students answer.)

5. Live your life to the fullest. Don't waste your life. Celebrate each and every heartbeat!

In John 10:10 why did Jesus say He came to earth? (To give us abundant life.)

WARM UP

YOUR FAMILY TREE

Fill in the chart and then the statements.

Grandma	Grandpa	Grandma	Grandpa
(Dad's mom)	(Dad's dad)	(Mom's mom)	(Mom's dad)

Dad   Mom

Brothers and Sisters

Me

The hospital or city I was born in is:

....

....

....

My most unique relative is:

....

....

....

The family member who is most inspiring is:

....

....

....

 TEAM EFFORT

YOUR GRAVESTONE

The following may sound like a morbid activity but you will find it very meaningful. Write what you would like to have printed on your gravestone (even though the odds are you will live to be over 70 years of age). Sometimes when we think about what we want our lives to represent when we die, it is easier to set priorities to accomplish our desired goals.

Here's an example of what I would want to put on my gravestone: "Here is a man who walked in integrity. He was deeply committed to his family and friends and he was a positive influence for God's kingdom."

Now you try it.

....

....

....

....

....

....

....

....

....

....

....

....

....

TEAM EFFORT

GRIEF

Undoubtedly, if you haven't already, you will one day experience the excruciating pain and grief that come when a loved one dies.

grief (grēf), n. 1. Grief may be called a life-shaking sorrow over loss. 2. Grief is a dark, heavy thing, and hard to penetrate. 3. The core of the grief experience is anxiety.[1]

Here are a few points to remember about grief:

1. Grief is normal. You must grieve before you can go on with life. Never be afraid to cry or recognize your hurt. These feelings and emotions are normal.

2. Grief takes time. You will not get over your pain instantly. The dull ache will be with you for a long time.

3. Don't be afraid to talk about your hurt. As we talk and share our sorrows, we at times receive strength and mutual support.

4. There is comfort. Read Scriptures of peace, hope and victory over death. Here are a few to look up:

> Psalm 23
> Psalm 46
> John 14
> Romans 8

5. You can be a comfort to others. Read this beautiful illustration of comfort that Joseph Bayly writes about in his helpful book, *The View from a Hearse*. One of his children had died and this is how he received comfort:

"I was sitting, torn by grief. Someone came and talked to me of God's dealing, of why it happened, of hope beyond the grave. He talked constantly, he said things I knew were true. I was unmoved, except to wish he'd go away. He finally did.

"Another came and sat beside me. He didn't talk. He didn't ask leading questions. He just sat beside me for an hour and more, listened when I said something, answered briefly, prayed simply, left. I was moved. I was comforted. I hated to see him go."[2]

Notes

1. Haddon W. Robinson, *Grief* (Grand Rapids: Christian Medical Society).

2. Ibid.

ON DEATH AND DYING

1. Life is a gift. Since our very breath and lives are a gift from God, our attitudes should be that of thankfulness to God.

Read the following verses and discuss how they relate to life being a gift to you from God:
Psalm 118:24
Psalm 150:2,6
Romans 5:8

2. Life is eternal. Life on earth is but a snap of the fingers compared to eternity. As we go about living our lives, the element of eternal life is sometimes forgotten.

What does the Bible say about eternal life?
John 3:16
1 John 2:25
1 John 5:13
After reading these Scriptures, what are your hopes, dream, fears, doubts and joys? Write your feelings in the space below and then share with your group.

....

....

3. There is hope! God brings hope to those with a fear of death.
Read John 14:1-3.

What words of reassurance and comfort does Jesus give His followers?

....

....

According to 2 Timothy 1:10 what is the good news of the gospel?

....

....

What is your "hope of glory" according to Colossians 1:27?

....

....

4. God walks with you. Read Psalm 23.

How can this psalm be a comfort to those who fear death?

....

....

Find at least two principles in this great psalm that will help remind you that God is with you.

....

....

IN THE WORD

5. Live your life to the fullest. Don't waste your life. Celebrate each and every heartbeat!

In John 10:10 why did Jesus say He came to earth?

....

....

....

6. Do not repress your fears about death and dying. Do you feel your fear of death and dying is normal? If you have never talked with someone about your fears do not be afraid to do so. There are no easy answers. However, there is someone near you with an understanding heart.

So What?

In the space provided below, write a prayer to God telling Him your greatest fears about death and dying. You may want to write about your fear of your own death or the death of a loved one. Write about your doubts of eternal life or about your thankfulness for the assurance of your salvation. After you have written about these feeling, talk with someone about your fears.

....

....

....

....

 Things to Think About

1. Why is it important to talk about our feelings concerning death?

....

....

....

2. How can our group encourage each other to be more honest with our feelings about death?

....

....

....

3. List some practical ways you could help when a special person in someone's life dies.

....

....

....

PARENT PAGE

The Ultimate Fear: The Fear of Death

The ultimate fear in life comes from the knowledge that we will one day die. Many people are so afraid of dying that they really never live life to the fullest. Some people repress their fear of death and act as though it will never happen to them.

The Ultimate Fact: We Will All Die

Let's read what the Bible has to say about the fact that we will all die.

What is the answer to the first question asked in Psalm 89:48?

....

....

....

What does Hebrews 9:27 say about the ultimate fact?

....

....

....

Why do you think people fear death?

....

....

....

In the space below, write your own thoughts about death. Write your fears, questions, hopes and any other thoughts you may have on this subject, and then share them with your family.

....

....

....

Session 4 "Death and Dying"
Date ....

MAJOR TRAUMA

LEADER'S PEP TALK

Can I be perfectly honest? This was not an easy section to write or frankly to give to kids. Any way you look at it, traumatic events in our lives are painful. I speak often on the trauma of sexual abuse. You'd think I would get used to the responses but I never do. As soon as I start the message and look out at the audience I always see a few heads drop, their eyes full of tears. The pain of their abuse is just too much for them to handle. Or when I talk about suicide or AIDS, someone always has experienced a loved one suffering with this kind of trauma. Again these subjects are just plain painful.

These aren't easy subjects but perhaps we in the Church have dodged them for far too long. We all learn and grow through tension, and I can't think of a better place for kids to talk about tension than in the love and security of their churches or Bible studies. My philosophy has always been Don't be afraid to bring up the difficult and traumatic issues from a Christian perspective, because if you don't, someone else will be glad to from a much more secular perspective.

You'll notice that in all four of these sessions I've put together lots of opportunities for discussion. Please don't forget that kids learn best when they talk, not when you talk. If you see your role as a coach and guide toward your students' self-discovery, then you are doing very effective work as a teacher. One young man came to me after I presented the session on pornography and said, " I had no idea I was even dabbling with pornography but I'm in it way over my head. No wonder my relationship with God has seemed so stale."

These sessions do two things that may seem like opposites. They bring up negative and traumatic issues and they provide another opportunity for you to present your students with hope. I want to remind you, so you will remind your precious students, that there is absolutely nothing that God can't handle. One of the great Christian leaders of a previous century was fond of saying, " I'm going to sleep now and I give God all my problems because He's going to be awake all night anyway."

One last suggestion. As you wade into what can be treacherous issues, don't be afraid to find resources and people who can come alongside you for encouragement, knowledge and counsel. If you need referrals or more help, feel free to call us at the National Institute of Youth Ministry. Our mission is to serve people like you who are "difference makers" in the lives of young people and their families. Thanks for caring for kids.

SEXUAL ABUSE

KEY VERSES

"For I am convinced that neither death nor life, neither angels nor demons, neither the present nor the future, nor any powers, neither height nor depth, nor anything else in all creation, will be able to separate us from the love of God that is in Christ Jesus our Lord."
Romans 8:38,39

BIBLICAL BASIS

Psalm 147:3-5;
Proverbs 11:14; 20:18;
John 11:17-37;
Romans 8:35-39

THE BIG IDEA

Sexual abuse is widespread in our society. If you or someone you know has been abused, it's absolutely necessary to get help and healing.

AIMS OF THIS SESSION

During this session you will guide students to:
• Examine the personal pain of sexual abuse;
• Discover what to do if they or their friends have been abused;
• Implement a decision to receive immediate help if they have been abused or to help someone who has been abused.

WARM UP

DON'T EVER GIVE UP—
A humorous view of persistence.

TEAM EFFORT— JUNIOR HIGH/ MIDDLE SCHOOL

WHAT IS SEXUAL ABUSE? (AND WHAT CAN YOU DO ABOUT IT?)—
Students examine the facts of sexual abuse.

TEAM EFFORT— HIGH SCHOOL

RAPE: QUESTIONS AND ANSWERS—
Students look at the abuse of rape.

IN THE WORD

HELP IN A HOPELESS SITUATION—
A Bible study on God's hope in abusive situations.

THINGS TO THINK ABOUT (OPTIONAL)

Questions to get students thinking and talking about sexual abuse.

PARENT PAGE

A tool to get the session into the home and allow parents and young people to discuss abuses.

LEADER'S DEVOTIONAL

"He heals the brokenhearted and binds up their wounds. He determines the number of the stars and calls them each by name. Great is our Lord and mighty in power; his understanding has no limit" (Psalm 147:3-5).

Every few months or so, Lori would come around when she needed help. My staff and I asked her how she was doing. The answer was always the same—and always a lie.

"Oh, things are going really good for me. I've got a job now and I'm staying at a friend's house. I'm doing really good with God."

The fact of the matter was that Lori wasn't doing good with God, anyone or anything. She was severely addicted to drugs and had already had an abortion or two. Though we tried to give assistance again and again for years, Lori would either run away or drop out of sight until she needed help again. How did this dark, sinister spiral of self-destruction begin? It all started when Lori was an innocent little girl.

When Lori was just a small child, her father began to systematically sexually abuse her and her older sisters. As a teenager, the sexual abuse continued along with physical violence. Though it sounds callous, Lori's abusive behavior towards herself was almost predictable. The seeds of her self-destruction began with sexual abuse.

According to sexual abuse statistics, you probably have a number of Loris in your youth ministry. Every student who experiences the trauma of sexual abuse won't turn into a tornado of self-destruction, but for every student like Lori, there are thousands more who silently suffer.

Educating young people about sexual abuse is a critical step for providing help to broken lives. Victims of sexual abuse need to know that there is help and healing in Jesus Christ. They need to know there are adults like you who care. Your compassion and unconditional love can help heal the unsightly scars of sexual abuse. You can be God's agent for help and freedom in Jesus Christ. (Written by Joey O'Connor.)

"Out of suffering have emerged the strongest souls; the most massive characters are sheared with scars."— E. H. Chapin

4. **God cares!** Frankly, most people who have experienced any kind of sexual abuse struggle with his or her relationship with God. Perhaps too many people spend their energies blaming God instead of being comforted by Him. He cares. He loves you and wants to heal your wounds. Read John 11:17-37. Although this story is about the death of a friend, there are numerous insights we can see that relate to how God cares for anyone who is hurting and how He offers hope.

What was the reaction of Jesus in verse 35? (He wept.)

Does this reaction surprise you? What does this tell you about Jesus? (Students answer.)

How would the conversation between Jesus and Martha in verses 23-25 be beneficial to a person who has been abused? (Students answer.)

Here's a difficult question. How can God care so deeply for a person who has been abused but still allow abuse to take place in our world? (Students answer.)

"Who shall separate us from the love of Christ? Shall trouble or hardship or persecution or famine or nakedness or danger or sword? As it is written: 'For your sake we face death all day long; we are considered as sheep to be slaughtered.' No, in all these things we are more than conquerors through him who loved us. For I am convinced that neither death nor life, neither angels nor demons, neither the present nor the future, nor any powers, neither height nor depth, nor anything else in all creation, will be able to separate us from the love of God that is in Christ Jesus our Lord" (Romans 8:35-39).

How could this wonderful promise make a difference in the life of someone who has been abused? (No matter what has happened to us in our lives, God will always love us and nothing can separate us from Him.)

So What?

If you or someone you know has been sexually abused, it is now time to seek the help needed to start the road to recovery. Seek help within the next 24 hours.

....

....

THINGS TO THINK ABOUT (OPTIONAL)

• Use the questions on page 107 after or as a part of "In the Word."

1. Why do you suppose the statistics for sexual abuse are getting higher and higher?

....

2. Why are people afraid to tell anyone about their abuses?

....

3. What role should God play in the life of a person who has been abused?

....

PARENT PAGE

• Distribute page to parents.

SEXUAL ABUSE

KEY VERSES

"For I am convinced that neither death nor life, neither angels nor demons, neither the present nor the future, nor any powers, neither height nor depth, nor anything else in all creation, will be able to separate us from the love of God that is in Christ Jesus our Lord." Romans 8:38,39

BIBLICAL BASIS

Psalm 147:3-5; Proverbs 11:14; 20:18; John 11:17-37; Romans 8:35-39

THE BIG IDEA

Sexual abuse is widespread in our society. If you or someone you know has been abused, it's absolutely necessary to get help and healing.

WARM UP (10-15 MINUTES)
DON'T EVER GIVE UP

• Divide students into groups of three or four.
• Give each student a copy of "Don't Ever Give Up" on page 95 and a pen or pencil, or display the page using an overhead projector.
• Have students complete the page and discuss.

What does this picture say about life?

When a person is expressing trouble, how can the advice "don't ever give up!" be beneficial?

Share one thing you are going through right now where this is good advice.

TEAM EFFORT—JUNIOR HIGH/ MIDDLE SCHOOL (10-15 MINUTES)
WHAT IS SEXUAL ABUSE? (AND WHAT CAN YOU DO ABOUT IT?)

• Give each student a copy of "What Is Sexual Abuse? (And What Can You Do About It?)"

— Fold —

on pages 97 and 99 and a pen or pencil, or display the page using an overhead projector.
• Have students complete the page.
• As a whole group discuss the page.

Now that you have this information, what are your thoughts, feelings and input?

Any questions?

If you or a friend of yours has been abused in any way, what would keep you from going to a leader with this information?

Why is bringing "the secret" into the open with a trusted adult counselor still the best decision to make?

TEAM EFFORT—HIGH SCHOOL (10-15 MINUTES)

RAPE: QUESTIONS AND ANSWERS

• Give each student a copy of "Rape: Questions and Answers" on page 101 and a pen or pencil, or display the page using an overhead projector.
• Have students complete the page and then discuss as a whole group.

Answers

1. B. Rape is forced sexual relations against a person's will. All victims of rape, regardless of their previous sexual experience, report rape as a violent and dangerous attack upon them that deeply affects their lives.

2. C. Rape is an act of power and aggression, NOT sex. Most men who rape have available sexual partners. Only about 3 percent of all convicted rapists are diagnosed as clinically "psychotic" or sick men. In a comparison study between rapists and nonrapists, there was no difference in personality profiles except for the tendency of the rapist to act out more aggressively, to be more accepting of the use of violence towards women and to be strongly accepting of traditional sex-role stereotypes.

3. False. Only about 50 percent of rapists use weapons (i.e., guns, knives, clubs, etc.). Rapists are more likely to use tricks, threats or physical force.

4. A. Most rapes are planned to some degree. About 50 percent of all rapes occur in the victims' homes during daylight hours.

5. C. Men who rape other men, for the most part, are NOT homosexual. They are straight men who are angry, hostile and violent. They rape men for the same reasons that they rape women—to degrade, humiliate and terrorize.

6. A. The majority of offenders (50-80 percent) are acquaintances of the victims (i.e., dates, friends, relative or neighbors). Oftentimes, acquaintance rape is much more devastating than stranger rape because the victim has entrusted her safety to this person and that safety is betrayed when she is raped.

7. C. No one asks to be raped. Rape is getting hurt and no asks to get hurt. Hitchhiking is a risky situation where rape can happen. However, no one hitchhikes intending to get raped. The way people dress has nothing to do with getting raped. In fact, most teenage

victims were wearing jeans when they were attacked.

8. False. Rapists do not have a "look." Any man, given an immature attitude toward women, a lack of respect for people in general and the inability to empathize with how another human feels, can be a rapist. That includes an uncle, father, next-door neighbor or a stranger.

9. A. The majority of rape victims are between the ages of 15 and 19. Some possible reasons are: this age group tends to be out of the home more often, whether alone or with a group of same-sex friends; this age may tend to be more vulnerable to threat or peer pressure for saying no to sexual coercion.

10. C. Most rapist are under 35 years old. The majority of reported rapists are between 15 and 24 years of age.

11. False. Statistics show that there are no more false reports of rape than there are for any other crime. Most rape victims do not even report the crime.

12. False. Rape victims are of all ages, shapes and descriptions. They come from all races. They are rich and poor. They can be male or female. It can happen to anyone. It can happen to you.

IN THE WORD (25-30 MINUTES)

HELP IN A HOPELESS SITUATION

• Give each student a copy of "Help in a Hopeless Situation" on pages 103 and 105 and a pen or pencil, or display the page using an overhead projector.
• As a whole group, complete the Bible study.

The statistics are staggering when it comes to sexual abuse. If you or a friend of yours has been sexually abused, here are four important and life-transforming points. At one time or another everyone you know will need to consider these points for either a friend or, unfortunately, for themselves.

If You've Been Sexually Abused....

1. It's not your fault. It's always the fault of the abuser. The abuser is sick. If you blame yourself, you will get sick also. A lot of people partly blame themselves for the sexual abuse. Why is it healthy to realize it's the fault of the abuser?

What kinds of sickness could come from abuse? (Physical, spiritual, emotional.)

2. Seek help. Don't suffer in silence. Most people who have been sexually abused are afraid to tell anyone. However, you can't get better without help. Your pain won't go away by itself.

If you were abused, who would you talk with about this problem?

Read Proverbs 11:14 and 20:18. Although these verses are talking about a nation at war, how would this advice be good for a person whose life is at war with the abuse that has been forced upon him or her?

What are the results of seeking help?

What are the results of remaining silent?

3. There is hope. Unfortunately millions have been abused. However, many people have sought help, worked through their pain and are now living happy lives.

Consider 17-year-old Annette. She is in your youth group. There is a lot of pain in her life from a sexual abuse situation years ago. Sometimes she does fine, but very near the surface of her life is the ever present feelings of grief from the sexual abuse.

As a group, bombard her with hope. Give her Scripture, help her see that God is present. Convince her that seeking help will benefit her in the long run. (You may want to role-play the situation with one of the adult leaders playing Annette.)

WARM UP

DON'T EVER GIVE UP

What does this picture say about life?

....
....
....

When a person is expressing trouble, how can the advice "don't ever give up!" be beneficial?

....
....
....

Share one thing you are going through right now where this is good advice.

....
....
....

Don't Ever Give Up

SEXUAL ABUSE

WHAT IS SEXUAL ABUSE? (AND WHAT CAN YOU DO ABOUT IT?)[1]

The sexual assault of a person occurs when a male or female tricked, coerced, seduced, intimidated, manipulated into cooperating or forced into not offering any resistance to sexual activity with another person.

Sexual abuse can be defined as:
- Showing children pornographic materials
- Taking nude pictures
- An adult exposing himself to a child or asking the child to expose himself or herself
- Fondling private areas of the body
- Intimate kissing
- Genital contact
- Intercourse
- Rape

Sexual assault includes incest, molestation, rape and "date rape."

Incest is sexual activity between any relatives.

Usually:	father/stepfather
	grandfather
	uncle
	cousin
	brother
Occasionally:	mother
	grandmother
	aunt

Molestation is sexual activity with someone outside the person's family. Eighty percent of molestations are by someone the victim knows and trusts:

family friend	mother's boyfriend
neighbor	teacher
coach	doctor/dentist
pastor/priest	youth leader
camp counselor	baby-sitter

Only 20 percent of molestations are perpetrated by strangers.

Rape is forced penetration (by penis or any object) of the vagina, mouth or anus against the will of the victim.

Acquaintance rape or "date rape" is rape by someone you know or are dating. Date rapists generally use just enough force to gain compliance. A man may use his physical power to coerce intercourse, taking advantage of a situation by using force, pressure, deception, trickery or teen vulnerability. The date rapist is not a weird, easily identifiable person. He is just like anyone else—except that he uses force to get his way.

About 75 percent of teen rapes are acquaintance or "date rapes."

SEXUAL ABUSE

TEAM EFFORT

What to Do If You Are Raped:

- Get to a safe place.
- Do not bathe, douche or change clothes.
- Call a rape crisis hotline.
- Have a friend or family member go with you to the hospital emergency room (take a change of clothes if possible):
- To preserve the evidence (very important if you decide to prosecute);
- To determine injury;
- To check for venereal disease and pregnancy.

Reporting the crime to police is a decision that only you can make.

Reasons for Reporting

Making a police report will benefit you directly.

- Reporting the assault is a way of regaining your sense of personal power and control;
- Reporting enables you to do something concrete about the crime committed against you;
- Reporting helps ensure that you receive the most immediate and comprehensive assistance available.

Making a police report will help prevent other people from being raped:

- Reporting and prosecuting the assailant are essential to the prevention of rape;
- Most rapists are repeat offenders;
- If the rape is not reported, the assailant cannot be apprehended.

Now that you have this information, what are your thoughts, feelings and input?

....

....

Any questions?

....

....

If you or a friend of yours has been abused in any way, what would keep you from going to a leader with this information?

....

....

Why is bringing "the secret" into the open with a trusted adult counselor still the best decision to make?

....

....

Note

1. Jim Burns, *Surviving Adolescence* (Dallas: Word Publishing, 1990), pp.143-145. Used by permission.

RAPE: QUESTIONS AND ANSWERS

1. Rape is
   a. Impossible without a woman's consent
   b. Forced sexual relations against a person's will.
   c. Not such a terrible experience.

2. Reasons men rape
   a. Sexually starved
   b. Crazy
   c. To overpower and humiliate other people

3. Guns or knives are usually used in rapes. True or False?

4. The place rape usually happens
   a. Home
   b. Woods
   c. Dark alleys

5. The majority of people who rape men are
   a. Gangs of oversexed women.
   b. Homosexual men.
   c. Heterosexual men or gangs of heterosexual men.

6. Most people are raped by
   a. People they know.
   b. Strangers.

7. People are asking to be raped when they are
   a. Hitchhiking.
   b. Wearing sexy clothing.
   c. None of the above.

8. You can tell if someone might be a rapist by looking at him. True or False?

9. The age of most rape victims is
   a. 15-19.
   b. 24-30.
   c. 35-50.

10. The age of most rapists is
    a. 65 and older.
    b. 35-65.
    c. 35 and younger.

11. Women often accuse innocent men of rape. True or False?

12. Only young, beautiful, sexy women are raped. True or False?

SEXUAL ABUSE

IN THE WORD

HELP IN A HOPELESS SITUATION

The statistics are staggering when it comes to sexual abuse. If you or a friend of yours has been sexually abused, here are four important and life-transforming points. At one time or another everyone you know will need to consider these points for either a friend or, unfortunately, for themselves.

If You've Been Sexually Abused...

1. It's not your fault. It's always the fault of the abuser. The abuser is sick. If you blame yourself, you will get sick also.

A lot of people partly blame themselves for the sexual abuse. Why is it healthy to realize it's the fault of the abuser?

....

....

What kinds of sickness could come from abuse?

....

....

2. Seek help. Don't suffer in silence. Most people who have been sexually abused are afraid to tell anyone. However, you can't get better without help. Your pain won't go away by itself.

If you were abused, who would you talk with about this problem?

....

Read Proverbs 11:14 and 20:18. Although these verses are talking about a nation at war, how would this advice be good for a person whose life is at war with the abuse that has been forced upon him or her?

....

....

What are the results of seeking help?

....

....

What are the results of remaining silent?

....

....

SEXUAL ABUSE

IN THE WORD

3. There is hope. Unfortunately millions have been abused. However, many people have sought help, worked through their pain and are now living happy lives.

Consider 17-year-old Annette. She is in your youth group. There is a lot of pain in her life from a sexual abuse situation years ago. Sometimes she does fine, but very near the surface of her life is the ever present feelings of grief from the sexual abuse.

As a group, bombard her with hope. Give her Scripture, help her see that God is present. Convince her that seeking help will benefit her in the long run. (You may want to role-play the situation with one of the adult leaders playing Annette.)

4. God cares! Frankly, most people who have experienced any kind of sexual abuse struggle with his or her relationship with God. Perhaps too many spend their energies blaming God instead of being comforted by Him. He cares. He loves you and wants to heal your wounds. Read John 11:17-37. Although this story is about the death of a friend, there are numerous insights we can see that relate to how God cares for anyone who is hurting and how He offers hope.

What was the reaction of Jesus in verse 35?

....

....

Does this reaction surprise you? What does this tell you about Jesus?

....

....

How would the conversation between Jesus and Martha in verses 23-25 be beneficial to a person who has been abused?

....

....

Here's a difficult question. How can God care so deeply for a person who has been abused but still allow abuse to take place in our world?

....

....

"Who shall separate us from the love of Christ? Shall trouble or hardship or persecution or famine or nakedness or danger or sword? As it is written: 'For your sake we face death all day long; we are considered as sheep to be slaughtered.' No, in all these things we are more than conquerors through him who loved us. For I am convinced that neither death nor life, neither angels nor demons, neither the present nor the future, nor any powers, neither height nor depth, nor anything else in all creation, will be able to separate us from the love of God that is in Christ Jesus our Lord" (Romans 8:35-39).

How could this wonderful promise make a difference in the life of someone who has been abused?

....

....

So What?

If you or someone you know has been sexually abused, it is now time to seek the help needed to start the road to recovery. Seek help within the next 24 hours.

THINGS TO THINK ABOUT

1. Why do you suppose the statistics for sexual abuse are getting higher and higher?

....

....

....

2. Why are people afraid to tell anyone about their abuses?

....

....

....

3. What role should God play in the life of a person who has been abused?

....

....

....

PARENT PAGE

A. Cheryl and Jack are both in the church youth group. After experiencing a youth group meeting on sexual abuse, they confide in your family that yes, they have been sexually abused.

As a family, what can you do to help them with their pain?

....

B. Read together through the following Helpful Hints for Ministering to the Sexually Abused:

Helpful Hints for Ministering to the Sexually Abused[1]

1. Provide security—The abuse victims need to feel safe and know they can trust you. Find a regular time to talk, listen and celebrate together.

2. Affirmation—Sexually abused persons have a poor self-concept ridden with guilt. They need acceptance.

3. Sense of belonging—Include the persons, even though their outward behavior appears distrustful. They need a safe support group that accepts them just the way they are.

4. Intimacy in appropriate ways—Share something about yourself, develop little "in" jokes, use eye contact. It's best not to touch a sexual abuse victim, for a touch may cause a flashback. When you've established a good relationship, you may ask the person if he or she minds a hand on the shoulder.

5. Encouragement—Without being patronizing, continue to encourage, support and stretch abuse victims to reach out again when they are ready.

6. Friendship—Find times just to be friends without the subject always centering around abuse. Have a Coke after school; go to an athletic event; see a movie.

7. Help them keep a positive, hopeful attitude about their life, family, future.

8. Find support groups in your community where they can get help and encouragement from others with the same experience.

9. Pray and share God's love with them in concrete ways.

Any questions or thoughts on this section?

....

C. Family Prevention Contract
What can you do to help prevent sexual abuse in your family?

....

Who can you talk with in a confidential manner if a problem ever arises with any type of abuse?

....

If a family member ever shares a traumatic sexual abuse experience we will NOT: preach, judge or condemn. Rather we will do everything we possibly can to serve, comfort and empower.

Signed	**Date**
....	....
....	....
....	....

Note

1. Lee Hovel, "Sexual Abuse: The Screaming Secret" *Group* (January, 1985): 12. Used by permission.

Session 5 "Sexual Abuse"
Date ....

SUICIDE

KEY VERSE

"The Lord is my light and my salvation—whom shall I fear? The Lord is the stronghold of my life—of whom shall I be afraid?" Psalm 27:1

BIBLICAL BASIS

Deuteronomy 31:8;
Psalm 27:1;
Isaiah 40:28-31

THE BIG IDEA

Suicide is a permanent solution to a temporary problem. God is the great provider of hope.

AIMS OF THIS SESSION

During this session you will guide students to:

• Examine the facts and issues of suicide;

• Discover the biblical principle of hope and how it relates to suicide;

• Implement a plan for considering options other than suicide when they feel depressed.

WARM UP
YOUR SUM TOTAL—
Students add up their assets.

TEAM EFFORT— JUNIOR HIGH/ MIDDLE SCHOOL
THE FACTS OF SUICIDE—
Students discuss the reality of suicide.

TEAM EFFORT— HIGH SCHOOL
THE TORMENTED REBEL KILLS HIMSELF—
A look at a victim of suicide.

IN THE WORD
HANG ON TO HOPE—
A Bible study on the hope found in God.

THINGS TO THINK ABOUT (OPTIONAL)

Questions to get students thinking and talking about taking suicide seriously.

PARENT PAGE

A tool to get the session into the home and allow parents and young people to discuss myths and facts regarding suicide.

LEADER'S DEVOTIONAL

"Do you not know? Have you not heard? The Lord is the everlasting God, the Creator of the ends of the earth. He will not grow tired or weary, and his understanding no one can fathom. He gives strength to the weary and increases the power of the weak. Even youths grow tired and weary, and young men stumble and fall; but those who hope in the Lord will renew their strength. They will soar on wings like eagles; they will run and not grow weary, they will walk and not be faint" (Isaiah 40:28-31).

Todd and I stood next to Phil's bed in South Coast Hospital's Intensive Care Unit. Connected to his body, tubes ran in every which way. Black charcoal lined his mouth and nostrils. Monitors beeped and hummed.

Every few minutes, Phil's body writhed and squirmed as he mumbled and groaned in agony. An ICU nurse walked through the door and someone asked how many pills Phil had swallowed.

"Over 40," came her curt reply.

Phil wasn't a high school student. Neither was he in junior high. Phil was a college student, one of our volunteer junior high leaders. Attempted suicide? Over 40 Advil? Didn't anyone see this one coming? How'd we miss this?

Those are questions Todd, our high school pastor, and I had to wrestle with as we contemplated the severity of Phil's attempted suicide. As suicide usually does, Phil's attempt to end his life caught everyone off guard.

One of the most useful ways to keep suicide from catching you or your students off guard is by understanding the importance of suicide prevention. How many teenage suicide attempts could be prevented if every teenager had someone to talk to? You are in the unique position to help kids in crisis. You are "standing in the gap" for today's teenagers. You will probably never know how many tragedies have been averted by your presence in young people's lives.

This lesson will give you the tools you need to understand the facts about suicide, how to help students talk about suicide, and clarify the many myths about suicide. Most importantly, it gives young people an action plan for understanding and dealing with their own feelings of suicide. It will help them help their friends in crisis and provide you an opportunity to minister to those students on the verge of becoming the next Phil. (Written by Joey O'Connor.)

"If God has made your cup sweet, drink it with grace; if He has made it bitter, drink it in communion with Him."— Oswald Chambers

SUICIDE

KEY VERSE

"The Lord is my light and my salvation—whom shall I fear? The Lord is the stronghold of my life—of whom shall I be afraid?" Psalm 27:1

BIBLICAL BASIS

Deuteronomy 31:8; Psalm 27:1; Isaiah 40:28-31

THE BIG IDEA

Suicide is a permanent solution to a temporary problem. God is the great provider of hope.

WARM UP (10-15 MINUTES)

YOUR SUM TOTAL

• Divide the students into groups of equal numbers.
• Give each group a pencil and a sheet of paper.
• Read aloud the following directions:
   Add the total score of the following:
   Team members' shoe sizes added together (one foot only).
   One point for each letter of each team member's last name.
   Points for hair color: blonde=2 points; brown=1 point; red=5 points; black=3 points; gray=10 points; white=10 points; green=25 points; other colors=25 points.
   One point for each different birth state represented by your team.
   One point for each sibling (brother or sister) of your team members.

TEAM EFFORT—JUNIOR HIGH/MIDDLE SCHOOL (10-15 MINUTES)

THE FACTS OF SUICIDE

• Divide students into groups of three or four.
• Give each student a copy of "The Facts of Suicide" on page 115 and a pen or pencil, or display the page using an overhead projector.
• Have students complete the page then discuss.

SO WHAT?

Even if you aren't feeling down right now, the odds say that one day you will need to hang on to hope. List three people you could go to when you need hope.

1. ....
2. ....
3. ....

Who can you give hope to this next week?

....

What specifically will you do to offer them hope?

....

THINGS TO THINK ABOUT (OPTIONAL)

• Use the questions on page 121 after or as a part of "In the Word."

1. Authorities on suicide say to take all discussions about suicide seriously. Why?

....

2. If a person told you that he or she was going to attempt suicide and had a time, a place and a method, what would you do?

....

3. Suicide is a permanent solution to a temporary problem. Why do so many young people continue to do it?

....

PARENT PAGE

• Distribute page to parents.

• Every year about 2 million teens attempt suicide.
• Seven thousand teens actually kill themselves.
• Suicide is in the top 5 percent of death causes for teens.
• Seventy-three percent of teens have thought about suicide and 27 percent of teens have tried it.
• One out of four teens have harbored serious thoughts of suicide this year.
• Seven out of 10 teens know someone who has attempted suicide.

These aren't fun statistics. Suicide is scary. Suicide is permanent.

How do those statistics make you feel?

....

Why do you think people look at suicide as a solution to their problems?

....

At your school these statistics seem:
☐ About right

☐ More than what actually happens. Why?

....

☐ Less than what actually happens. Why?

....

"Suicide is a permanent solution to a temporary problem." What do you think of this statement?

....

TEAM EFFORT—HIGH SCHOOL (10-15 MINUTES)

THE TORMENTED REBEL KILLS HIMSELF

• Divide students into groups of three or four.
• Give each student a copy of "The Tormented Rebel Kills Himself" on page 117 and a pen or pencil, or display the page using an overhead projector.
• Have students complete the page then discuss.

Kurt Cobain: His Fans Mourn His Passing

Once again the rock world was shaken by the suicide death of one of its most gifted artists of the 1990s, Kurt Cobain of the rock group Nirvana. In life, Cobain was often in pain. His songs often told of the void in his heart. The rock world knows of the self-destructive streak in Cobain. He had been addicted to heroin, and fled a drug rehabilitation center in California days before his death in Seattle, Washington. Cobain, like so many mega rock stars before him (Jimi Hendrix, Jim Morrison), decided life was not worth living.

114

---- Fold ----

One student in Connecticut said, "I just have a feeling that our generation is dying away. There's Kurt and River Phoenix. The aimless quality of my age. The job situation. I think a lot of people think they're not understood, that parents don't understand them, that society has no place for them because of their age." That might help explain why suicide already ranks as the third-leading killer of high school students.

1. What do you think caused Kurt Cobain to commit suicide?

....

2. What circumstances in his life contributed to his decision?

....

3. Imagine you have five minutes to try talking Kurt Cobain out of killing himself. What would you say?

....

IN THE WORD (25-30 MINUTES)

HANG ON TO HOPE

• Give each student a copy of "Hang on to Hope" on page 119 and a pen or pencil, or display the page using an overhead projector.
• As a whole group, complete the Bible study.
1. "The Lord is my light and my salvation—whom shall I fear? The Lord is the stronghold of my life—of whom shall I be afraid?" (Psalm 27:1).
Even in the midst of life's most disturbing times, the Scripture is clear—there is always hope. Fill in this piece of paper with hopeful phrases.

....

2. It's Friday, but Sunday's Comin'.
Tony Campolo often tells a story of a great African-American pastor preaching a simple message to his congregation—"It's Friday, but Sunday's comin'." The theme is of course taken from the death (Friday) and resurrection (Sunday) of Jesus. The death and resurrection of Jesus is a cornerstone of hope. Friday represents the negative issues, disease, broken relationships, depression, anger, sin and pain. Sunday represents new life, new blessings, forgiveness, freedom, peace and joy.
Take a few moments to write down your problems under Friday and the hopeful solutions under Sunday.

Friday	Sunday

3. "He will never leave you nor forsake you" (Deuteronomy 31:8). Whenever we are feeling despair, we can be comforted by this hope-filled promise of God, that He will not leave or forsake us.
What does this verse mean to you? (Students answer.)

 **TEAM EFFORT**

THE FACTS OF SUICIDE

- Every year about 2 million teens attempt suicide.
- Seven thousand teens actually kill themselves.
- Suicide is in the top 5 percent of death causes for teens.
- Seventy-three percent of teens have thought about suicide and 27 percent of teens have tried it.
- One out of four teens have harbored serious thoughts of suicide this year.
- Seven out of 10 teens know someone who has attempted suicide.[1]

These aren't fun statistics. Suicide is scary. Suicide is permanent.

How do those statistics make you feel?

....

....

Why do you think people look at suicide as a solution to their problems?

....

....

At your school these statistics seem:

☐ About right.

....

....

☐ More than what actually happens. Why?

....

....

☐ Less than what actually happens. Why?

....

....

"Suicide is a permanent solution to a temporary problem." What do you think of this statement?

....

....

....

Note

1. Statistics are from the Hotline Help Center in Anaheim, California, and the Center for Disease Control in Atlanta, Georgia.

SUICIDE

THE TORMENTED REBEL KILLS HIMSELF

Kurt Cobain: His Fans Mourn His Passing

Once again the rock world was shaken by the suicide death of one of its most gifted artists of the 1990s, Kurt Cobain of the rock group Nirvana. In life, Cobain was often in pain. His songs often told of the void in his heart. The rock world knows of the self-destructive streak in Cobain. He had been addicted to heroin, and fled a drug rehabilitation center in California days before his death in Seattle, Washington. Cobain, like so many mega rock stars before him (Jimi Hendrix, Jim Morrison), decided life was not worth living.

One student in Connecticut said, "I just have a feeling that our generation is dying away. There's Kurt and River Phoenix. The aimless quality of my age. The job situation. I think a lot of people think they're not understood, that parents don't understand them, that society has no place for them because of their age." That might help explain why suicide already ranks as the third-leading killer of high school students.

1. What do you think caused Kurt Cobain to commit suicide?

....

....

....

2. What circumstances in his life contributed to his decision?

....

....

....

3. Imagine you have five minutes to try talking Kurt Cobain out of killing himself. What would you say?

....

....

....

# IN THE WORD

SUICIDE

HANG ON TO HOPE

1. "The Lord is my light and my salvation—whom shall I fear? The Lord is the stronghold of my life—of whom shall I be afraid?" (Psalm 27:1).
Even in the midst of life's most disturbing times, the Scripture is clear—*there is always hope*. Fill in this piece of paper with hopeful phrases.

....

....

2. It's Friday, but Sunday's Comin'.
Tony Campolo often tells a story of a great African-American pastor preaching a simple message to his congregation—"It's Friday, but Sunday's comin'." The theme is of course taken from the death (Friday) and resurrection (Sunday) of Jesus. The death and resurrection of Jesus is a cornerstone of hope.

Friday represents the negative issues, disease, broken relationships, depression, anger, sin and pain. Sunday represents new life, new blessings, forgiveness, freedom, peace and joy.
Take a few moments to write down your problems under Friday and the hopeful solutions under Sunday.

<u>Friday</u>	<u>Sunday</u>
....	....
....	....
....	....

3. "He will never leave you nor forsake you" (Deuteronomy 31:8). Whenever we are feeling despair, we can be comforted by this hope-filled promise of God, that He will not leave or forsake us.
What does this verse mean to you?

....

....

SO WHAT?

Even if you aren't feeling down right now, the odds say that one day you will need to hang on to hope. **List three people you could go to when you need hope.**
1. ....
2. ....
3. ....

Who can you give hope to this next week?

....

What specifically will you do to offer them hope?

....

....

SUICIDE

HINGS TO THINK ABOUT

1. Authorities on suicide say to take all discussions about suicide seriously. Why?

....

....

....

2. If a person told you that he or she was going to attempt suicide and had a time, a place and a method, what would you do?

....

....

....

3. Suicide is a permanent solution to a temporary problem. Why do so many young people continue to do it?

....

....

....

PARENT PAGE

MYTHS OF SUICIDE

• People who talk about suicide won't do it. Wrong—Eighty percent of suicide victims talked about it, but friends and family didn't take it seriously.

• Mentioning suicide to a friend in crisis may give him or her the idea. Wrong—Actually talking about suicide can help the friend see what others think about it also.

• Suicide occurs without warning. Wrong—Unfortunately hindsight is easier than foresight but usually there are warning signs such as withdrawal, the giving away of prized possessions, a difficult romantic breakup and heavy use of drugs and alcohol to deaden the pain.

• All suicidal people are mentally ill. Wrong—Only 15 percent of those who commit suicide have actually been diagnosed as mentally ill.

• Suicidal people are totally committed to dying. Wrong—One of their most common characteristics is ambivalence toward life and death.

• When the depression lifts, the suicide crisis is over. Wrong—Often the abrupt lifting of the depression suggests that they have finally decided to end their lives.

• Suicidal people do not seek medical help. Wrong—Strangely enough three out of four sought medical help in the last three months of their lives.

THE SUICIDE QUESTIONNAIRE[1]

Here's a quick questionnaire that provides a suicidal potential evaluation based on a person's self-rating. Each family member can take this and then discuss any issues that come up.

	Yes	No
1. My future happiness looks promising.	___	___
2. I have recently had difficulty sleeping.	___	___
3. I think I am to blame for almost all my trouble.	___	___
4. When I'm sick, the doctor often prescribes sedatives for me.	___	___
5. My future looks secure.	___	___
6. Sometimes I fear I will lose control over myself.	___	___
7. Sometimes I really feel afraid.	___	___
8. Lately I haven't felt like participating in my usual activities.	___	___
9. I go on occasional drinking sprees.	___	___
10. In the last few years I have moved at least twice.	___	___
11. I have someone whose well-being I care about very much.	___	___
12. I generally feel that I am completely worthless.	___	___
13. I frequently have a drink in the morning.	___	___

Suicidal counselees will tend to produce the following pattern of responses:

1. No   6. Yes   10. Yes
2. Yes   7. Yes   11. No
3. Yes   8. Yes   12. Yes
4. Yes   9. Yes   13. Yes
5. No

"Greater is he that is in you, than he that is in the world" (1 John 4:4, *KJV*).

How is this verse meaningful to anyone who would be contemplating suicide?

....
....
....

Note

1. Jim Burns, *The Youth Builder* (Eugene, Oreg.: Harvest House, 1988), pp. 270-271. Used by permission.

Session 6 "Suicide" Date.................................

AIDS

KEY VERSE

"If one part suffers, every part suffers with it." 1 Corinthians 12:26

BIBLICAL BASIS

Exodus 3:1-10;
Psalm 23:4;
Matthew 17:15;
Romans 5:3;
1 Corinthians 6:19; 12:26

THE BIG IDEA

AIDS requires a biblical response from all Christians.

AIMS OF THIS SESSION

During this session you will guide students to:

- Examine the risks and dangers of the HIV and AIDS;
- Discover a biblical approach to AIDS and suffering;
- Implement a plan to assist those suffering from AIDS.

WARM UP
HIV AND AIDS AT RISK STATEMENTS—

Students express their opinions regarding risk levels for the HIV and AIDS.

TEAM EFFORT— JUNIOR HIGH/ MIDDLE SCHOOL
AIDS: A CURSE OR NATURAL CONSEQUENCE?—

Students debate AIDS-related issues.

TEAM EFFORT— HIGH SCHOOL
HELPING SOMEONE WITH THE HIV OR AIDS—

A look at someone who is HIV positive.

IN THE WORD
WHAT CAN WE LEARN ABOUT SUFFERING?—

A Bible study on God's view of those who suffer.

THINGS TO THINK ABOUT (OPTIONAL)

Questions to get students thinking and talking about AIDS.

PARENT PAGE

A tool to get the session into the home and allow parents and young people to discuss the facts regarding AIDS.

LEADER'S DEVOTIONAL

"Even though I walk through the valley of the shadow of death, I will fear no evil, for you are with me; your rod and your staff, they comfort me" (Psalm 23:4).

Though AIDS is getting less attention in the media than it used to, AIDS continues to ravage the lives of millions. As your students sit in public schools and receive blatant lectures on condom use and the myths about so-called safe sex, extensive studies have demonstrated that young people aren't listening. The condom campaign has been shunned as quickly as their parents' advice telling them not to have sex before marriage. Kids today are sick of hype and hypocrisy. If they are going to choose abstinence before marriage, they need strong, solid reasons why.

Challenging young people with God's call for sexual abstinence before marriage is the best prevention against AIDS and the host of sexually transmitted diseases a teenager can contract in a few moments of sexual pleasure. Though AIDS is a hideous, deadly disease, so far it is not preventing young people from being sexually active. Yes, even the possibility of death will not prevent some people from sexual activity.

That's why I believe young people need a higher standard for living. Teenagers need a higher reason for remaining sexually pure. You have the awesome opportunity to call young people to sexual purity. You have the privilege of presenting God's plan for living a holy and pleasing life to Him.

AIDS is a weak motivator for sexual purity. It is God alone who can motivate young people with a desire for sexual purity. Following His standard for their lives, teenagers can receive all the grace and strength they need to glorify God with their bodies.

At the same time that you help young people with sexual purity, you can teach them how to handle the AIDS crisis with the compassion of Jesus Christ. Serving AIDS victims in the name of Jesus is the compassionate response to this terrible trauma that this world needs. (Written by Joey O'Connor.)

"I'm scared to die such a young man. I'd like a little more time. I lived in the fast lane. If only God will give me a break."—28-year-old victim of AIDS, *Time* Magazine

AIDS

KEY VERSE

"If one part suffers, every part suffers with it." 1 Corinthians 12:26

BIBLICAL BASIS

Exodus 3:1-10; Psalm 23:4; Matthew 17:15; Romans 5:3; 1 Corinthians 6:19; 12:26

THE BIG IDEA

AIDS requires a biblical response from all Christians.

WARM UP (10-15 Minutes)

HIV and AIDS at Risk Statements

- Give each student a copy of "HIV and AIDS at Risk Statements" on page 129 and a pen or pencil, or display the page using an overhead projector.
- Have students complete the page.

For each statement choose either "Agree," "Disagree" or "Undecided" and then discuss your response.

- Young people who experiment with cigarettes, alcohol, sex and drugs could be in danger of getting the HIV.
- A child who tries a cigarette in the fourth or fifth grade will likely try riskier behavior later.
- Girls who develop physically at an early age could be more at risk because they may unwittingly attract older men, yet lack the maturity or social skills to protect themselves from unwelcome advances.
- Adolescents who have serious problems in school are at risk because they possibly lack self-esteem and are likely to be tempted by drugs, alcohol or sex in order to feel good about themselves.
- Impoverished teens in inner cities are in a special risk category because, more than likely, tremendous drug activity takes place in their neighborhoods, and there is far more pressure to use drugs and have sex at an early age.

(The correct answer to all of these statements is "Agree.")

TEAM EFFORT—JUNIOR HIGH/ MIDDLE SCHOOL (10-15 Minutes)

AIDS: A Curse or Natural Consequence?

- Give each student a copy of "AIDS: A Curse or Natural Consequence?" on page 129 and a pen or pencil, or display the page using an overhead projector.

--- Fold ---

Divide into two groups and debate the issues of AIDS using these statements:
1. AIDS is a curse from God, or AIDS is a natural consequence of our fallen world.
2. AIDS victims should not be allowed to live in public, or AIDS victims should receive all the freedoms of anyone else.
3. A doctor with AIDS should quit his or her medical practice immediately, or A doctor with AIDS has the same rights as any other doctor.
4. A teacher with AIDS should quit teaching students, or A teacher with AIDS may continue to teach as long as he or she is healthy.
5. Homosexuality is a worse sin than adultery or fornication, or Homosexuality is no different than adultery or fornication.

TEAM EFFORT—HIGH SCHOOL (10-15 Minutes)

HELPING SOMEONE WITH THE HIV OR AIDS

• Divide students into groups of three or four.
• Give each student a copy of "Helping Someone with the HIV or AIDS" on page 131 and a pen or pencil, or display the page using an overhead projector.
• Have students complete the page.

Julie is a beautiful 17-year-old who attends your youth group at church. You have recently become friends but you haven't known each other for very long. One night after the youth-group meeting she tells you this story: "I've told no one yet but three weeks ago I found out I'm HIV positive. My parents don't know, our youth workers don't know and no other friends know. When I was 14, I had one sexual contact with a guy I barely knew. It was my only experience. After I found out I had the HIV, I tried to find him. He died of AIDS four months ago."

What can you do to help Julie?
....
....
....

Where is God in the midst of Julie's suffering?
....
....

What are her issues?
....
....
....

IN THE WORD (25-30 Minutes)

What Can We Learn About Suffering?

• Have a narrator read Exodus 3:1-10 and have other students act out the events in this account. You may assign the roles before the session. Students may use props and/or costumes.
• Give each student a copy of "What Can We Learn About Suffering?" on page 133 and a pen or pencil, or display the page using an overhead projector.

• As a whole group, complete the Bible study.
What can we learn from Exodus 3:1-10 about God's relationship to our suffering? (See v. 7.) (God understands our misery. He hears our cries. He is concerned about our suffering.)
What principles can we learn about suffering from these three Scriptures?
Principle One—1 Corinthians 12:26 (In the Body of Christ, if one member suffers, all members suffer.)
Principle Two—Matthew 17:15 (God has mercy on the suffering.)
Principle Three—Romans 5:3 (Suffering produces perseverance. Find the joy and good in the situation.)
In what ways does God care about the suffering of people with AIDS? (Students answer.)

SO WHAT?

Given the reality of AIDS, the suffering of those who have AIDS and the suffering of their loved ones, what three actions will you take?
1. ....
2. ....
3. ....

THINGS TO THINK ABOUT (OPTIONAL)

• Use the questions on page 135 after or as a part of "In the Word."
1. Why is it important to get the straight facts on AIDS?
....
2. What can Christians do for people who have AIDS?
....
3. What do you think God thinks about people with AIDS?
....

PARENT PAGE

• Distribute page to parents.

Fold

AIDS

WARM UP

HIV AND AIDS AT RISK STATEMENTS[1]

For each statement choose either "Agree," "Disagree" or "Undecided" and then discuss your response.

- Young people who experiment with cigarettes, alcohol, sex and drugs could be in danger of getting the HIV.
- A child who tries a cigarette in the fourth or fifth grade will likely try riskier behavior later.
- Girls who develop physically at an early age could be more at risk because they may unwittingly attract older men, yet lack the maturity or social skills to protect themselves from unwelcome advances.
- Adolescents who have serious problems in school are at risk because they possibly lack self-esteem and are likely to be tempted by drugs, alcohol or sex in order to feel good about themselves.
- Impoverished teens in inner cities are in a special risk category because, more than likely, tremendous drug activity takes place in their neighborhoods, and there is far more pressure to use drugs and have sex at an early age.

Note

1. Information is paraphrased from the article by Mary-Ann Shafer, M.D., and Florence Isaacs, "Teenagers and AIDS," *Good Housekeeping*, May 1990. This was featured in the monthly health column "The Better Way."

TEAM EFFORT

AIDS: A CURSE OR NATURAL CONSEQUENCE?[1]

Divide into two groups and debate the issues of AIDS with these statements:

1. AIDS is a curse from God, *or* AIDS is a natural consequence of our fallen world.
2. AIDS victims should not be allowed to live in public, *or* AIDS victims should receive all the freedoms of anyone else.
3. A doctor with AIDS should quit his or her medical practice immediately, *or* A doctor with AIDS has the same rights as any other doctor.
4. A teacher with AIDS should quit teaching students, *or* A teacher with AIDS may continue to teach as long as he or she is healthy.
5. Homosexuality is a worse sin than adultery or fornication, *or* Homosexuality is no different than adultery or fornication.

Note

1. Jim Burns, *Radical Respect: A Christian Approach to Love, Sex and Dating* (Eugene, Oreg.: Harvest House Publications, 1992), pp.169-170. Used by permission.

AIDS

TEAM EFFORT

HELPING SOMEONE WITH THE HIV OR AIDS

Julie is a beautiful 17-year-old who attends your youth group at church. You have recently become friends but you haven't known each other for very long. One night after the youth-group meeting she tells you this story: "I've told no one yet but three weeks ago I found out I'm HIV positive. My parents don't know, our youth workers don't know and no other friends know. When I was 14, I had one sexual contact with a guy I barely knew. It was my only experience. After I found out I had the HIV, I tried to find him. He died of AIDS four months ago."

What can you do to help Julie?

....

....

....

What are her issues?

....

....

....

Where is God in the midst of Julie's suffering?

....

....

....

AIDS

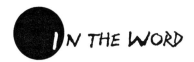

WHAT CAN WE LEARN ABOUT SUFFERING?

What can we learn from Exodus 3:1-10 about God's relationship to our suffering? (See v. 7.)

....

....

....

What principles can we learn about suffering from these three Scriptures?

Principle One—1 Corinthians 12:26

....

....

Principle Two—Matthew 17:15

....

....

Principle Three—Romans 5:3

....

....

In what ways does God care about the suffering of people with AIDS?

....

....

SO WHAT?

Given the reality of AIDS, the suffering of those who have AIDS and the suffering of their loved ones, what three actions will you take?

1. ....

   ....

2. ....

   ....

3. ....

   ....

   ....

AIDS

THINGS TO THINK ABOUT

1. Why is it important to get the straight facts on AIDS?

....

....

....

2. What can Christians do for people who have AIDS?

....

....

....

3. What do you think God thinks about people with AIDS?

....

....

....

AIDS

ARENT PAGE

QUESTIONS AND ANSWERS ABOUT AIDS[1]

As a family, review these questions and answers on AIDS. Make sure everyone understands the facts.

• What does AIDS stand for?

Acquired **I**mmune **D**eficiency **S**yndrome

• What is AIDS?

A fatal disease that attacks the immune system, leaving the victim's body defenseless to illnesses that it can normally fight off such as pneumonia and meningitis.

• How do you get AIDS?

Mostly by having sex with an infected person or by sharing needles and syringes used to inject illegal drugs. The virus is present in the blood, semen, and vaginal secretions. It can be transmitted from one homosexual partner to another, or from a man to a woman or a woman to a man during sexual intercourse or oral sex. The virus can enter the body through sores in the mouth and microscopic tears in the tissue of sex organs.

• How else is AIDS transmitted?

Some victims were exposed to the AIDS virus through blood they have received in a transfusion. Since the start of careful blood screening tests, this rarely occurs now. About a third of the babies born to mothers with AIDS are infected.

• Can you get AIDS from shaking hands, hugging, kissing, coughing, sneezing, or eating food prepared by someone with AIDS? Can you get it through masturbation, toilet seats, door knobs, or insect bites?

No known cases have been transmitted in any of these ways.

• Can you get AIDS by having your ears pierced?

No one is known to have received it this way as yet, but it is conceivable. If you are having this done, insist on a sterile needle.

• Can you get AIDS from someone who doesn't know he or she has it?

Yes. This is usually what happens. Because it sometimes takes five years (and possibly longer) after exposure for symptoms to appear, most carriers don't discover they have it until they have already passed it on.

• Can you be infected with the AIDS virus and never get AIDS?

Yes. Between one-fourth and one-half of those infected with the virus will develop AIDS within four to ten years. Some say that the percentage is more like one-half to two-thirds.

• How can I protect myself from getting AIDS?

Wait until marriage before having sex. When you have sex with someone, you are having sex with everyone he or she has had sex with for the past 10 years.

• Where can I find out more about AIDS?

Your local Red Cross office carries information, as do local and state health departments.

Now that you've looked at the questions and answers, are there any questions you have about the disease?

....

....

....

What practical steps can everyone in the family take to not be at risk of this disease?

....

....

....

....

....

How does this verse fit this discussion?

"Do you not know that your body is a temple of the Holy Spirit, who is in you, whom you have received from God?" (1 Corinthians 6:19).

....

....

....

....

....

Note

1. Todd Temple, *Hot Buttons II* (Ventura, Calif.: Regal Books, 1987), pp. 15-17. Used by permission.

Session 7 "AIDS"

Date..

PORNOGRAPHY

KEY VERSE

"The body is not meant for sexual immorality, but for the Lord, and the Lord for the body."
1 Corinthians 6:13

BIBLICAL BASIS

Genesis 1:26,27;
Matthew 25:40;
1 Corinthians 6:9,10,13;
Ephesians 4:18,19;
Colossians 3:5,12,14;
1 Thessalonians 4:4-7·
1 Timothy 6:10.

THE BIG IDEA

Pornography is anti-God, antisex, antiwomen and antichildren. Pornography attacks our very souls and is addicting.

AIMS OF THIS SESSION

During this session you will guide students to:

• Examine the harmful effects of pornography;
• Discover how dangerous pornography is to their spiritual, physical, emotional and mental health;
• Implement decisions and safeguards to keep them from the problems associated with pornography.

WARM UP

MY FAVORITES—
Students tell their favorites.

TEAM EFFORT— JUNIOR HIGH/ MIDDLE SCHOOL

WHERE DO YOU FIND PORNOGRAPHY?—
The facts regarding the availability of pornography.

TEAM EFFORT— HIGH SCHOOL

HOW MUCH DO YOU KNOW ABOUT PORNOGRAPHY AND ITS EFFECTS?—
Students look at the truth of pornography.

IN THE WORD

THE BATTLE AGAINST PORNOGRAPHY—
A Bible study on the effects of pornography.

THINGS TO THINK ABOUT(OPTIONAL)

Questions to get students thinking and talking about pornography.

PARENT PAGE

A tool to get the session into the home and allow parents and young people to discuss staying free from pornography.

LEADER'S DEVOTIONAL

"Each of you should learn to control his own body in a way that is holy and honorable, not in passionate lust like the heathen, who do not know God; and that in this matter no one should wrong his brother or take advantage of him. The Lord will punish men for all such sins, as we have already told you and warned you. For God did not call us to be impure, but to live a holy life" (1 Thessalonians 4:4-7).

Kevin had been active in his church's middle school ministry for more than three years. An excellent musician, the students loved how he jammed on the guitar. Kevin was a friendly, easygoing leader who spent hour after hour with young junior highers. He was popular and eager to help out, and loads of kids looked up to him.

Kevin had a strong love for God and young people. What he appeared to be on the outside, however, deceptively hid his secret life on the inside.

The shock came when police investigators arrived at Kevin's church to ask the junior and senior high pastors about his suspicious behavior. To their horror, disbelief and sadness, Kevin was being indicted for trafficking pornographic material. He was a link in a major pornography ring. His secret life was publicly exposed.

Pornography destroys lives. It destroys the lives of every person exposed to its addictive tentacles. It degrades and cheapens those made in God's image. It violates those who make it, those who watch it and the innocent victims who suffer its destructive effects. Pornography kills the human spirit because it seeks to possess and manipulate what God has made holy. Pornography kills the joy-filled life God intended for every person. It is a wildfire of destruction.

You can help young people deal with their sexuality in a positive way by helping them understand the dangers of pornography. Pornography is rarely talked about in the church, but there are thousands of young people who struggle with what they read and watch on TV. You can assist young people to make pacts of purity by exposing pornography for what it is. This lesson will help you expose the dangers of pornography. (Written by Joey O'Connor.)

"Though debased, pornography is a theological statement. It says: There is no God who says I should limit my lust or channel my passion or give as well as get....Pornography is anti-woman and anti-child. It is anti-marriage and anti-permanence. Thus it is profoundly anti-civilization. Since civilization is social support to the dynamics of life, pornography is anti-life."—William Stanmeyer

PORNOGRAPHY

Fold

EY VERSE

"The body is not meant for sexual immorality, but for the Lord, and the Lord for the body."
1 Corinthians 6:13

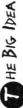IBLICAL BASIS

Genesis 1:26,27; Matthew 25:40; 1 Corinthians 6:9,10,13; Ephesians 4:18,19; Colossians 3:5,12,14; 1 Thessalonians 4:4-7; 1 Timothy 6:10

THE BIG IDEA

Pornography is anti-God, antisex, antiwomen and antichildren. Pornography attacks our very soul and is addicting.

WARM UP (10-15 MINUTES)

MY FAVORITES

- Divide students into groups of three or four.
- Have students complete the following statements.
- As a whole group, develop an all-time favorite list.

My favorite TV show is:
My favorite song is:
My favorite music group is:
My favorite book is:
My favorite magazine is:
My favorite movie is:

TEAM EFFORT—JUNIOR HIGH/ MIDDLE SCHOOL (10-15 MINUTES)

WHERE DO YOU FIND PORNOGRAPHY?

- Divide students into groups of three or four.
- Give each student a copy of "Where Do You Find Pornography?" on page 143 and a pen or pencil, or display the page using an overhead projector.
- Have students complete the page.

How is pornography actually an attack on God? (Students answer.)
Why do you think pornography tends to exploit women and children? (Students answer.)

5. Pornography and greed are partners in evil.

Pornography and greed feed upon each other. The pornography industry takes advantage of people for personal gain, regardless of the destructive impact. Both producer and seller reap huge profits due to exorbitant markups.

Greed is displeasing to God and destructive to humankind. God exhorts in His Word that we live by honest labor and that "the love of money is a root of all kinds of evil" (1 Timothy 6:10).

What are the motives of the pornography industry? (Primarily to make money.)
What does "the love of money is a root of all kinds of evil" actually mean? (Students answer.)

6. Pornography destroys normal human relationships.

Pornography dictates that the satisfaction of one's own desires is all that matters. It leaves in its wake broken marriages, estranged and molested children, shattered young people and deterioration of neighborhoods.

Jesus taught that we are our brother's keeper. In fact, we are accountable to each other: "Put to death, therefore, whatever belongs to your earthly nature: sexual immorality, impurity, lust, evil desires and greed....clothe yourselves with compassion, kindness, humility, gentleness and patience....And over all these virtues put on love, which binds them all together in perfect unity" (Colossians 3:5,12,14).

How is pornography anti-God sexuality? (Students answer.)

SO WHAT?

As a group, come up with a group "mission statement" about pornography. Then ask the group to consider signing this mission statement as its commitment to a pornography-free lifestyle.

....

THINGS TO THINK ABOUT (OPTIONAL)

- Use the questions on page 151 after or as a part of "In the Word."

1. Do you believe pornography can be addictive?

....

2. What do experts mean when they say that one of the harmful effects of pornography is "the power of the picture"?

....

3. What are several practical ways to keep away from pornography?

....

PARENT PAGE

- Distribute page to parents.

TEAM EFFORT—HIGH SCHOOL (10-15 Minutes)

How Much Do You Know About Pornography and Its Effects?

- Divide students into groups of three or four.
- Give each student a copy of "How Much Do You Know About Pornography and Its Effects?" on page 145 and a pen or pencil, or display the page using an overhead projector.
- Have students complete the page.

1. A woman is raped in the United States every
    a. 46 seconds.   **b. 5 minutes.**   **c. 8 minutes.**

(A woman is raped in the United States every 46 seconds.)

2. The most frequent users of pornography are
    a. men over the age of 30.
    b. boys between the ages of 12 and 17.
    c. men between the ages of 18 and 25.

(Boys between the ages of 12 and 17 are the most frequent users of pornography.)

3. There are more hardcore pornography outlets in this country than McDonald's restaurants. True False

(True.)

4. In a lifetime, the typical serial child molester abuses more than
    a. 25 victims.   **b. 100 victims.**   **c. 360 victims.**

(The typical serial child molester abuses more than 360 children in his or her lifetime. Both adult and child pornography is often used as an aid during the crime.)

5. Sexually transmitted diseases strike more children per year than polio did in the 11-year epidemic between 1942 and 1953.   True   False

(True.)

6. More than 80 percent of those who sexually abuse children admit to regular use of pornography. True False

(True. More than 80 percent of those who sexually abuse children do admit to regular use of pornography, often imitating actual scenes during the abuse.)

7. The pornography distribution capital of the world is
    a. Amsterdam.   **b. Los Angeles.**   **c. Bangkok.**

(Southern California [Los Angeles] is the distribution capital of the world, housing 39 of the 47 major producers of pornography.)

8. Pornography is a 75-million-dollar-a-year business.   True   False

(False. Pornography is an 8- to 10-billion-dollar-a-year business.)

9. Since 1960 in the United States, the rape rate has increased   a. 25 percent.   b. 500 percent.   c. 75 percent.

(Since 1960 the rape rate in the United States has increased 500 percent.)

10. According to the FBI, after drugs and gambling, illegal pornography is the _____ leading source of revenue for organized crime.   **a. 3rd**   **b. 10th**   **c. 20th**

(According to the FBI, illegal pornography is the third leading source of revenue for organized crime.)

11. _____ American girls will be molested by the time they are 18 years old.
    a. One out of 10   **b. One out of 25**   **c. One out of 3**

(One out of 3 American girls will be sexually molested by the age of 18.)

12. In California, possession of child pornography is a misdemeanor and not a felony.   True   False

(True.)

13. Only _____ percent of rape victims will ever see their attackers caught or imprisoned.
    a. 2   **b. 10**   **c. 25**

(The Senate Judiciary Committee issued a report noting that only 2 percent of rape victims will see their attackers caught or imprisoned. Fifty-four percent of rape cases end in acquittals or are dismissed before trial. Less than half of those arrested for rape are convicted, compared to 68 percent convicted for murder, and 61 percent convicted for robbery.)

14. There are more than _____ child molesters residing in this country.
    a. 500,000   **b. 1 million**   **c. 4 million**

(There are 4 million child molesters in the United States.)

Answers are provided by "Enough Is Enough Campaign," an affiliate of the National Coalition Against Pornography.

IN THE WORD (25-30 Minutes)

THE BATTLE AGAINST PORNOGRAPHY

- Give each student a copy of "The Battle Against Pornography" on pages 147, 149 and 151 a pen or pencil, or display the page using an overhead projector.
- As a whole group, complete the Bible study.

1. Pornography destroys the image of God in people.

Read Genesis 1:26,27.

What does this passage mean? (We were created in God's image. Since we are made in God's image, every human being is worthy of honor and respect.)

How can pornography destroy the image of God in others? (Students answer.)

2. Pornography is addictive.

How can pornography become addictive? (Students answer.)

What parts of Ephesians 4:18,19 describe addictive behavior? (Always indulging in impure behavior and always lusting for more, never satisfied.)

Pornography subtly winds around its users an ever-tightening chain of bondage to the impulses and potential extravagance of sexual instincts. The apostle Paul describes this process as the "hardening of their hearts. Having lost all sensitivity, they have given themselves over to sensuality so as to indulge in every kind of impurity, with a continual lust for more" (Ephesians 4:18,19).

3. Pornography is anti-Christian.

Pornography openly mocks the most precious truths of our faith: the person of Jesus Christ, the Lord's supper and the Crucifixion. It mocks and belittles marital fidelity, morality and commitment to family life. God abhors all that is immoral, idolatrous, sexually perverted and lustful.

"Do not be deceived: Neither the sexually immoral nor idolaters nor adulterers...will inherit the kingdom of God....The body is not meant for sexual immorality, but for the Lord, and the Lord for the body" (1 Corinthians 6:9,10,13).

How does pornography take something as beautiful as our sexuality created by God and turn it into something so against the very nature of God? (Students answer.)

4. Pornography attacks women and children.

Pornography exploits and dehumanizes women as discardable tools for the satisfaction of male lust, and children are abused mentally, emotionally, physically and spiritually to satisfy the hedonistic urges of abusers.

Christianity ascribes a special place of honor to women and children. Through centuries when neither were looked upon with favor by pagan society, God's Word gave them dignity and value.

Conscientious followers of Christ dare not turn their backs on such destructive behavior. Child-destroyers are enemies of God! "Whatever you did for one of the least of these brothers of mine, you did for me" (Matthew 25:40).

Fold

PORNOGRAPHY

TEAM EFFORT

WHERE DO YOU FIND PORNOGRAPHY?

I. The Facts
- Ninety-nine out of 100 guys have looked at pornographic materials.[1]
- Nine out of 10 girls answer yes to viewing pornography.[2]
- Some studies tell us that at least 50 percent of the teenage population in America views something pornographic each month.[3]
- The primary consumers of pornographic materials are male adolescents between the ages of 12 and 17.[4]
- There are more stores selling pornographic material than McDonald's restaurants.[5]

II. The Top Ten Pornographic Distributors
Brainstorm at least 10 places where it is easy to find pornography.

1. ....   6. ....

2. ....   7. ....

3. ....   8. ....

4. ....   9. ....

5. ....   10. ....

Now brainstorm what you can do as individuals and as a group to break the chain of the negative addictive behavior of viewing pornography.

....

....

....

Notes

1. Adapted from Connie Neal, "Your Teenager's Fascination With Pornography" *Parents of Teenagers* (June-July 1991): 8.

2. Ibid.

3. Jerry Kirk, "A Winnable War" (Cincinnati, Ohio: National Coalition on Pornography, 1989).

4. Neal, "Your Teenager's Fascination with Pornography," 8.

5. Bob DeMoss, "How Kids Get Hooked on Porn" *Group* (October, 1993): 32.

PORNOGRAPHY

TEAM EFFORT

HOW MUCH DO YOU KNOW ABOUT PORNOGRAPHY AND ITS EFFECTS?

1. A woman is raped in the United States every

a. 46 seconds.   b. 5 minutes.   c. 8 minutes.

2. The most frequent users of pornography are

a. men over the age of 30.

b. boys between the ages of 12 and 17.

c. men between the ages of 18 and 25.

3. There are more hardcore pornography outlets in this country than McDonald's restaurants.

True   False

4. In a lifetime, the typical serial child molester abuses more than

a. 25 victims.   b. 100 victims.   c. 360 victims.

5. Sexually transmitted diseases strike more children per year than polio did in the 11-year epidemic between 1942 and 1953.

True   False

6. More than 80 percent of those who sexually abuse children admit to regular use of pornography.

True   False

7. The pornography distribution capital of the world is

a. Amsterdam.   b. Los Angeles.   c. Bangkok.

8. Pornography is a 75-million-dollar-a-year business.

True   False

9. Since 1960 in the United States, the rape rate has increased

a. 25 percent.   b. 500 percent.   c. 75 percent.

10. According to the FBI, after drugs and gambling, illegal pornography is the _____ leading source of revenue for organized crime.

a. 3rd   b. 10th   c. 20th

11. _____ American girls will be molested by the time they are 18 years old.

a. One out of 10   b. One out of 25   c. One out of 3

12. In California, possession of child pornography is a misdemeanor and not a felony.

True   False

13. Only _____ percent of rape victims will ever see their attackers caught or imprisoned.

a. 2   b. 10   c. 25

14. There are more than _____ child molesters residing in this country.

a. 500,000   b. 1 million   c. 4 million

IN THE WORD

THE BATTLE AGAINST PORNOGRAPHY[1]

1. Pornography destroys the image of God in people.
Read Genesis 1:26,27.
What does this passage mean?

....

....

How can pornography destroy the image of God in others?

....

....

2. Pornography is addictive.
Pornography subtly winds around its users an ever-tightening chain of bondage to the impulses and potential extravagance of sexual instincts. The apostle Paul describes this process as the "hardening of their hearts. Having lost all sensitivity, they have given themselves over to sensuality so as to indulge in every kind of impurity, with a continual lust for more" (Ephesians 4:18,19).
How can pornography become addictive?

....

....

What parts of Ephesians 4:18,19 describe addictive behavior?

....

....

3. Pornography is anti-Christian.
Pornography openly mocks the most precious truths of our faith: the person of Jesus Christ, the Lord's supper and the Crucifixion. It mocks and belittles marital fidelity, morality and commitment to family life. God abhors all that is immoral, idolatrous, sexually perverted and lustful.

"Do not be deceived: Neither the sexually immoral nor idolaters nor adulterers ...will inherit the kingdom of God....The body is not meant for sexual immorality, but for the Lord, and the Lord for the body" (1 Corinthians 6:9,10,13).
How does pornography take something as beautiful as our sexuality created by God and turn it into something so against the very nature of God?

....

....

4. Pornography attacks women and children.
Pornography exploits and dehumanizes women as discardable tools for the satisfaction of male lust, and children are abused mentally, emotionally, physically and spiritually to satisfy the hedonistic urges of abusers.

Christianity ascribes a special place of honor to women and children. Through centuries when neither were looked upon with favor by pagan society, God's Word gave them dignity and value.

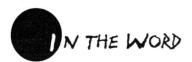

IN THE WORD

Conscientious followers of Christ dare not turn their backs on such destructive behavior. Child-destroyers are enemies of God!

"Whatever you did for one of the least of these brothers of mine, you did for me" (Matthew 25:40).

How is pornography actually an attack on God?

....

....

Why do you think pornography tends to exploit *women* and *children?*

....

....

5. Pornography and greed are partners in evil.

Pornography and greed feed upon each other. The pornography industry takes advantage of people for personal gain, regardless of the destructive impact. Both producer and seller reap huge profits due to exorbitant markups.

Greed is displeasing to God and destructive to humankind. God exhorts in His Word that we live by honest labor and that "the love of money is a root of all kinds of evil" (1 Timothy 6:10).

What are the motives of the pornography industry?

....

....

What does "the love of money is a root of all kinds of evil" actually mean?

....

....

6. Pornography destroys normal human relationships.

Pornography dictates that the satisfaction of one's own desires is all that matters. It leaves in its wake broken marriages, estranged and molested children, shattered young people and deterioration of neighborhoods.

Jesus taught that we are our brother's keeper. In fact, we are accountable to each other: "Put to death, therefore, whatever belongs to your earthly nature: sexual immorality, impurity, lust, evil desires and greed,....clothe yourselves with compassion, kindness, humility, gentleness and patience....And over all these virtues put on love, which binds them all together in perfect unity" (Colossians 3:5,12,14).

How is pornography anti-God sexuality?

....

....

SO WHAT?

As a group, come up with a group "mission statement" about pornography. Then ask the group to consider signing this mission statement as its commitment to a pornography-free lifestyle.

....

....

....

....

....

....

....

....

Note

1. Adapted from Jerry D. Kirk, *What the Bible Says—Ten Reasons Why You Should Get Involved in the Fight Against Pornography* (Colorado Springs: Focus on the Family, 1989), p. 3-5. Used by permission.

THINGS TO THINK ABOUT

1. Do you believe pornography can be addictive?

....

....

....

2. What do experts mean when they say that one of the harmful effects of pornography is "the power of the picture"?

....

....

....

3. What are several practical ways to keep away from pornography?

....

....

....

PARENT PAGE

PORNOGRAPHY AND SCRIPTURE

Read each verse or passage and then put in your own words how this section of Scripture might relate to pornography.

1 Corinthians 6:9-13

....

Ephesians 4:18,19

....

Ephesians 5:11

....

Philippians 4:8

....

Colossians 3:5-14

....

What are your thoughts? "There has not been a sex murder in the history of our department in which a killer was not an avid reader of lewd magazines."—Herbert Case, former Detroit Police Inspector

....

....

What can you do to keep youselves a pornography-free family? Discuss each area and come up with your own family guidelines.

Music

....

TV

....

Movies

....

Magazines

....

Books

....

Pictures

....

Other

....

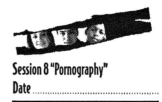

Session 8 "Pornography"

Date ....

MAJOR STRESSES

LEADER'S PEP TALK

This section is where the rubber meets the road. It's about taking our Christian faith into the inner struggles of our everyday lives. I don't know about you but there is many a day when I feel like I'm alone. I worry about all the plates I'm spinning. When I'm under pressure I have to watch it or I become a little moody. And when I'm moody and feel stress coming on, you should see me put down those chocolate chip cookies. Then I look at my stomach and oh, do I feel lonely, worried and moody. At times that's the real me.

I love this story from an old children's book called *The Velveteen Rabbit*.

The Skin Horse had lived longer in the nursery than any of the others. He was so old that his brown coat was bald in patches and showed the seams underneath, and most of the hairs on his tail had been pulled out to string bead necklaces. He was wise, for he had seen a long succession of mechanical toys arrive to boast and swagger, and by-and-by break their mainsprings and pass away, and he knew that they were only toys, and would never turn into anything else. For nursery magic is very strange and wonderful, and only those playthings that are old and wise and experienced like the Skin Horse understand all about it.

"What is REAL?" asked the Rabbit one day, when they were living side by side near the nursery fenders, before Nana came to tidy the room. "Does it mean having things that buzz inside you and a stick-out handle?"

"Real isn't how you are made," said the Skin Horse. "It's a thing that happens to you. When a child loves

you for a long, long time, not just to play with, but REALLY loves you, then you become Real."

"Does it hurt?" asked the rabbit.

"Sometimes," said the Skin Horse, for he was always truthful. "When you are Real, you don't mind being hurt."

"Does it happen all at once, like being wound up," he asked, "Or bit by bit?"

"It doesn't happen all at once," said the Skin Horse. "You become. It takes a long time. That's why it doesn't often happen to people who break easily, or have sharp edges, or who have to be carefully kept. Generally, by the time you are Real, most of your hair has been loved off, and your eyes drop out and you get loose in the joints and very shabby. But these things don't matter at all, because once you are Real, you can't be ugly, except to people who don't understand."[1]

Being real. I believe there is a refreshing new wind within many of our churches. Finally Christians are talking about being less than perfect and yet still striving to be God's people. Let's be honest. God wants to meet us where we are, not where we should be. When we struggle, the good news is that God is present.

As an influencer of kids, you can receive the same message that you are presenting in this material—God loves you just the way you are. So put away any pretenses, relax and get prepared to offer real answers to real inner struggles.

Note

1. Margery Williams, *The Velveteen Rabbit* (New York: Avon Books, 1975), pp. 16-17.

LONELINESS

KEY VERSE

"The Lord is my shepherd, I shall not be in want." Psalm 23:1

BIBLICAL BASIS

Deuteronomy 31:8;
Psalm 23;
Matthew 11:28,29;
Hebrews 10:25

THE BIG IDEA

At times, everyone feels the pain of loneliness. God is with you during times of loneliness.

AIMS OF THIS SESSION

During this session you will guide students to:
• Examine the fact that most people at times experience loneliness;
• Discover biblical principles for dealing with loneliness;
• Implement a plan to creatively deal with loneliness in a positive manner.

WARM UP

THE LONELY METER—
Students discuss times when they feel lonely.

TEAM EFFORT— JUNIOR HIGH/ MIDDLE SCHOOL

THOUGHTS ON LONELINESS—
Students share their thoughts regarding loneliness.

TEAM EFFORT— HIGH SCHOOL

DESPERATELY LONELY—
A look at a friend in great need.

IN THE WORD

WORKING THROUGH LONELINESS—
A Bible study on dealing with feelings of loneliness.

THINGS TO THINK ABOUT (OPTIONAL)

Questions to get students thinking and talking about dealing with loneliness.

PARENT PAGE

A tool to get the session into the home and allow parents and young people to discuss times of loneliness.

Leader's Devotional

"The Lord himself goes before you and will be with you; he will never leave you nor forsake you. Do not be afraid; do not be discouraged" (Deuteronomy 31:8).

When bringing on new volunteer staff members, I always try to find out what type of friendships the prospective volunteers have with their peers. My reason? Helping students develop healthy, positive friendships is most effective with a staff who has healthy, positive friendships of their own.

Too often, I've seen volunteer youth workers develop relationships with teenagers as a way to deal with loneliness. Youth workers who only have students for friends can create unhealthy relationships. Youth workers who put friendship before leadership can develop dangerous and dysfunctional youth ministries. Claiming spiritual answers to their social problems and using young people to boost their self-esteem, youth workers can deceive themselves into thinking they don't need meaningful peer relationships.

If you, a staff member or a student is experiencing loneliness, you can have hope that God walks with every person through the valley of loneliness. Don't allow working with kids to mask the loneliness in your heart. God is with you and your students through the pain and anxiousness that loneliness brings.

Everyone experiences loneliness at one time or another. The most effective way of dealing with loneliness is by developing a game plan to counter its ugly feeling and effects. This lesson will inspire you to handle personal loneliness in a positive manner and also, to help your students in a constructive, Christ-centered way. Jesus promises to never leave you nor forsake you. He will walk with you even when you don't feel His presence. His life will overshadow your loneliness with His love and grace. (Written by Joey O'Connor.)

"The best way to forget your own problems is to help someone else solve his."
—Anonymous

LONELINESS

KEY VERSE

KEY VERSE

"The Lord is my shepherd, I shall not be in want." Psalm 23:1

BIBLICAL BASIS

Deuteronomy 31:8; Psalm 23; Matthew 11:28,29; Hebrews 10:25

THE BIG IDEA

At times, everyone feels the pain of loneliness. God is with you during times of loneliness.

WARM UP (10-15 MINUTES)

THE LONELY METER

• Divide students into groups of three or four.
• Give each student a copy of "The Lonely Meter" on page 161 and a pen or pencil, or display the page using an overhead projector.
• Have students complete the page.

Give a number to each statement on the lonely meter (1 represents "not lonely at all" and 10 represents "extremely lonely"). Then discuss your answers.

"She told me she already had a date."

"He broke up with me on Friday and went out with her on Saturday."

"I feel like a lonesome loser!"

"We all went to the amusement park and had a pretty good time."

"We had the best talk."

"My Christmas was horrible—the first since my parents divorced. My dad went out drinking and my mom went on a date. I just sat home on Christmas all by myself."

TEAM EFFORT—JUNIOR HIGH/ MIDDLE SCHOOL (10-15 MINUTES)

THOUGHTS ON LONELINESS

• Divide students into groups of three or four.
• Give each student a copy of "Thoughts on Loneliness" on page 161 and a pen or pencil, or display the page using an overhead projector.
• Have students complete their pages.

---

5. Be creative when you are lonely. When you feel the lonely bug come over you, do something you enjoy: go for a walk, pray, read a good book, write a letter, read the Bible (Psalms and Proverbs can be especially helpful), treat yourself to a dessert or call a friend and have fun together.

Make a list of special things you like to do. Write down at least five.

a. ....

b. ....

c. ....

d. ....

e. ....

Keep this list handy. Next time you feel lonely, read through this list and do one or more of the things you have suggested.

6. Be others-centered.

We live in a me-first, I-centered society. Yet me-first, I-centered people are lonely. What can you do to be a more others-centered person? List at least five special service-oriented things you can do. Be as specific as possible (for example, bake cookies for Grandma, mow the lawn this afternoon, write an encouraging note today).

a. ....

b. ....

c. ....

d. ....

e. ....

7. Commit your loneliness to God.

Jesus said, "Come to me, all you who are weary and burdened, and I will give you rest. Take my yoke upon you and learn from me, for I am gentle and humble in heart, and you will find rest for your souls" (Matthew 11:28,29).

SO WHAT?

What are a few burdens that you need to take off your shoulders and place on the strong, sturdy shoulders of our Lord?

....

THINGS TO THINK ABOUT (OPTIONAL)

• Use the questions on page 171 after or as a part of "In the Word."

1. Some experts believe that each generation of people actually becomes more and more lonely. Do you believe this is true? Why?

....

2. Do you think Christ was ever lonely? Why or why not?

....

3. Why do you think Jesus gathered a group of close friends around Him?

PARENT PAGE

• Distribute page to parents.

True .... False .... The majority of people in my school are lonely most of the time.

True .... False .... Adults are more lonely than teenagers.

True .... False .... Loneliness causes people to lower their moral standards.

True .... False .... Some teenagers have sex, get pregnant and get married because they are basically lonely.

True .... False .... God will always cure your loneliness.

 TEAM EFFORT—HIGH SCHOOL (10-15 Minutes)

DESPERATELY LONELY

- Divide students into groups of three or four.
- Give each student a copy of "Desperately Lonely" on page 163 and a pen or pencil, or display the page using an overhead projector.
- Have students complete their pages.

Silva seldom seemed happy. Many times in the day she would just stare out in space for a while. Because she was often negative she didn't have many friends. She was a loner but almost seemed like she would rather be by herself than with others. At other times she seemed fine. Since her personality was on the quiet side no one expected her to be the "life of the party." In fact, some of the people thought she might be very "spiritual because they often saw her at lunch sitting alone reading her Bible.

One day she confided in her youth group that she was "desperately lonely." She didn't believe that anyone really liked her and, to be honest, she was sort of right! To make matters worse, she said her mom and dad were getting a divorce and were too caught up in their own problems to be of much help.

Is Silva's loneliness unhealthy?

Do you think Silva might also be depressed or suicidal?

What advice can you give her about her parents?

What could you do to help her through her loneliness? What could her youth group do?

Where does God fit into the picture?

 IN THE WORD (25-30 Minutes)

WORKING THROUGH LONELINESS

- Give each student a copy of "Working Through Loneliness" on pages 165, 167 and 169 a pen or pencil, or display the page using an overhead projector.
- As a whole group, complete the Bible study.

An Answer to Our Loneliness

"The Lord is my shepherd. I shall not be in want. He makes me lie down in green pastures, he leads me beside quiet waters, he restores my soul. He guides me in paths of righteousness for his name's sake. Even though I walk through the valley of the shadow of death, I will fear no evil, for you are with me; your rod and your staff, they comfort me. You prepare a table before me in the presence of my enemies. You anoint my head with oil; my cup overflows. Surely goodness and love will follow me all the days of my life, and I will dwell in the house of the Lord forever" (Psalm 23).

Circle words or phrases in this psalm that speak to you about working through loneliness. Then discuss in your group why these words or phrases caught your attention.

Working Through Loneliness
Here are seven statements about loneliness. Discuss each statement.

Action Steps
1. It's normal. In fact, it can be healthy.

When have you experienced loneliness in your life?

Has loneliness ever been a tool to lead you toward a more positive life? Why or why not?

2. Don't withdraw from everyone and everything.
"Let us not give up meeting together, as some are in the habit of doing, but let us encourage one another—and all the more as you see the Day approaching" (Hebrews 10:25).

What is the significance of this verse?

How can total withdrawal be destructive?

3. Move away from "crisis-mode living."
Definition: Crisis-mode living is when you spend most every waking moment of every day trying to figure out how to keep all the plates spinning. It's when we are overcommitted, too busy and stressed out.
What do you see as the results of crisis-mode living?
Busyness can sometimes feed our loneliness. What do you think of this phrase, "If the devil can't make you bad, he will make you busy?" (Students answer.)
How is Psalm 23 the opposite of crisis-mode living? (Students answer.)
4. Risk developing special friendships.
With whom would you like to become closer friends? List three or four names.

a.

b.

c.

d.

What specifically can you do with each individual in the next two weeks to strengthen the relationships (examples: lunch together, shopping, bike riding)?

WARM UP

THE LONELY METER

Give a number to each statement on the lonely meter (1 represents "not lonely at all" and 10 represents "extremely lonely"). Then discuss your answers.

...... "She told me she already had a date."

...... "He broke up with me on Friday and went out with her on Saturday."

...... "I feel like a lonesome loser!"

...... "We all went to the amusement park and had a pretty good time."

...... "We had the best talk."

...... "My Christmas was horrible—the first since my parents divorced. My dad went out drinking and my mom went on a date. I just sat home on Christmas all by myself."

TEAM EFFORT

THOUGHTS ON LONELINESS

True .... False .... The majority of people in my school are lonely most of the time.

True .... False .... Adults are more lonely than teenagers.

True .... False .... Loneliness causes people to lower their moral standards.

True .... False .... Some teenagers have sex, get pregnant and get married because they are basically lonely.

True .... False .... God will always cure your loneliness.

 **T**EAM **E**FFORT

DESPERATELY LONELY

Silva seldom seemed happy. Many times in the day she would just stare out in space for a while. Because she was often negative she didn't have many friends. She was a loner but almost seemed like she would rather be by herself than with others. At other times she seemed fine. Since her personality was on the quiet side no one expected her to be the "life of the party." In fact, some of the people thought she might be very spiritual because they often saw her at lunch sitting alone reading her Bible.

One day she confided in her youth group that she was "desperately lonely." She didn't believe that anyone really liked her and, to be honest, she was sort of right! To make matters worse, she said her mom and dad were getting a divorce and were too caught up in their own problems to be of much help.

Is Silva's loneliness unhealthy?

....

....

....

Do you think Silva might also be depressed or suicidal?

....

....

....

What advice can you give her about her parents?

....

....

....

What could you do to help her through her loneliness? What could her youth group do?

....

....

....

Where does God fit into the picture?

....

....

....

IN THE WORD

WORKING THROUGH LONELINESS

An Answer to Our Loneliness

"The Lord is my shepherd. I shall not be in want. He makes me lie down in green pastures, he leads me beside quiet waters, he restores my soul. He guides me in paths of righteousness for his name's sake. Even though I walk through the valley of the shadow of death, I will fear no evil, for you are with me; your rod and your staff, they comfort me. You prepare a table before me in the presence of my enemies. You anoint my head with oil; my cup overflows. Surely goodness and love will follow me all the days of my life, and I will dwell in the house of the Lord forever" (Psalm 23).

Circle words or phrases in this psalm that speak to you about working through loneliness. Then discuss in your group why these words or phrases caught your attention.

Working Through Loneliness

Here are seven statements about loneliness. Discuss each statement.

Action Steps

1. It's normal. In fact, it can be healthy.

When have you experienced loneliness in your life?

....

....

Has loneliness ever been a tool to lead you toward a more positive life? Why or why not?

....

....

2. Don't withdraw from everyone and everything.

"Let us not give up meeting together, as some are in the habit of doing, but let us encourage one another—and all the more as you see the Day approaching" (Hebrews 10:25).

What is the significance of this verse?

....

....

How can total withdrawal be destructive?

....

....

....

IN THE WORD

3. Move away from "crisis-mode living."

Definition: Crisis-mode living is when you spend most every waking moment of every day trying to figure out how to keep all the plates spinning. It's when we are overcommitted, too busy and stressed out.

What do you see as the results of crisis-mode living?

....

....

Busyness can sometimes feed our loneliness. What do you think of this phrase, "If the devil can't make you bad, he will make you busy?"

....

....

How is Psalm 23 the opposite of crisis-mode living?

....

....

4. Risk developing special friendships.

With whom would you like to become closer friends? List three or four names.

a...

b...

c...

d...

What specifically can you do with each individual in the next two weeks to strengthen the relationships (examples: lunch together, shopping, bike riding)?

5. Be creative when you are lonely. When you feel the lonely bug come over you, do something you enjoy: go for a walk, pray, read a good book, write a letter, read the Bible (Psalms and Proverbs can be especially helpful), treat yourself to a dessert or call a friend and have fun together.

Make a list of special things you like to do. Write down at least five.

a...

b...

c...

d...

e...

Keep this list handy. Next time you feel lonely, read through this list and do one or more of the things you have suggested.

 **N THE WORD**

6. Be others-centered.

We live in a me-first, I-centered society. Yet me-first, I-centered people are lonely. What can you do to be a more others-centered person? **List at least five special service-oriented things you can do. Be as specific as possible (for example, bake cookies for Grandma, mow the lawn this afternoon, write an encouraging note today).**

a. ....

b. ....

c. ....

d. ....

e. ....

7. Commit your loneliness to God.

Jesus said, "Come to me, all you who are weary and burdened, and I will give you rest. Take my yoke upon you and learn from me, for I am gentle and humble in heart, and you will find rest for your souls" (Matthew 11:28,29).

So What?

What are a few burdens that you need to take off your shoulders and place on the strong, sturdy shoulders of our Lord?

....

....

....

....

....

*T*HINGS TO THINK ABOUT

1. Some experts believe that each generation of people actually becomes more and more lonely. Do you believe this is true? Why?

....

....

....

2. Do you think Christ was ever lonely? Why or why not?

....

....

....

3. Why do you think Jesus gathered a group of close friends around Him?

....

....

....

 **PARENT PAGE**

LONELINESS AND THE FAMILY

I'm most lonely when:

....

....

....

You could help me when I'm lonely by:

....

....

....

I wouldn't get lonely if I could just:

....

....

....

A prayer request for me would be:

....

....

Jesus said, "Come to me, all you who are weary and burdened, and I will give you rest. Take my yoke upon you and learn from me, for I am gentle and humble in heart, and you will find rest for your souls. For my yoke is easy and my burden is light" (Matthew 11:28-30).

How does this Scripture relate to your family?

....

....

....

How can you experience this truth to a greater extent in your family?

....

....

....

Session 9 "Loneliness"
Date..

MOODINESS

KEY VERSE

"Do everything without complaining or arguing." Philippians 2:14

BIBLICAL BASIS

Psalm 143:7,8;
Matthew 6:25-34;
Philippians 2:14; 4:8

THE BIG IDEA

Many people have become consumed with moodiness. Much of our moodiness can be overcome as we recognize our reasons for becoming moody.

AIMS OF THIS SESSION

During this session you will guide students to:

- Examine what creates moodiness in their lives;
- Discover how to overcome some of their habits of moodiness;
- Implement more positive attitudes with more balanced approaches to life.

WARM UP

PET PEEVES—

Students express their feelings.

TEAM EFFORT— JUNIOR HIGH/ MIDDLE SCHOOL

NO-HELP HELPERS—

A skit on how to help someone in need.

TEAM EFFORT— HIGH SCHOOL

STRESS AND MOODINESS—

An inventory of some symptoms and causes of stress.

IN THE WORD

PUT LIFE IN PERSPECTIVE—

A Bible study on developing a proper perspective on life.

THINGS TO THINK ABOUT (OPTIONAL)

Questions to get students thinking and talking about being moody.

PARENT PAGE

A tool to get the session into the home and allow parents and young people to discuss stress in families.

LEADER'S DEVOTIONAL

"Answer me quickly, O Lord; my spirit fails. Do not hide your face from me or I will be like those who go down to the pit. Let the morning bring me word of your unfailing love, for I have put my trust in you. Show me the way I should go, for to you I lift up my soul" (**Psalm 143:7,8).**

Moody students can be some of the worst students in your youth ministry. They can whine. Pout. Complain. They even play that stupid silent game. Before you start pulling your hair out and consider skinning your moody nemeses alive, try to look at your students' problems in a bigger perspective.

Ask yourself, "What are their home lives like? Do they have any medical or developmental problems? Have they recently suffered any traumas or abuses? Were there particular events or situations that triggered their irritability?"

Moodiness is a dark river with many sources. The source of a particular student's moodiness can be as simple as a poor grade on a test or as serious as a life-threatening illness in his or her family. Whatever the source of his or her bad mood seems to be, it's an opportunity to love the student just as he or she is. When you love your students in good moods and bad, it builds trust in your relationships with them.

Students will have all sorts of sources for their moodiness, but you can challenge them to own their problems and to choose the attitudes they want to live by. It may also be helpful to examine what makes you moody, your pet peeves and sources of irritations. If you're feeling guilty for not liking a moody student, then you're not alone. Every youth minister has one or two students who drive him or her crazy.

If God wanted perfect youth ministers to love His kids into the Kingdom, He would have never chosen humans to be instruments of His grace. As it is, regardless of your moods, He's chosen to use you for His perfect work. Be encouraged! God wants to use you to love moody teenagers. (Written by Joey O'Connor.)

"Perhaps the greatest discovery of this century is that if you can change your attitude, you can change your life."
—William James

MOODINESS

EY VERSE

"Do everything without complaining or arguing." Philippians 2:14

IBLICAL BASIS

Psalm 143:7,8; Matthew 6:25-34; Philippians 2:14; 4:8

T HE BIG IDEA

Many people have become consumed with moodiness. Much of our moodiness can be overcome as we recognize our reasons for becoming moody.

W ARM UP (10-15 MINUTES)

PET PEEVES

• Divide students into groups of three or four.
• Have students complete the following statements:

My two greatest pet peeves are:

A major bummer for me is:

If I could change something about my family it would be:

When I become an adult, I will let teenagers:

If I was the person in charge I would:

T EAM EFFORT—JUNIOR HIGH/ MIDDLE SCHOOL (10-15 MINUTES)

NO-HELP HELPERS

• Ask for four volunteers to perform the skit "No-Help Helpers" on page 179.
• Give each performer a copy of "No-Help Helpers."
• As the skit is being performed, have the rest of the group think of words and phrases that describe how a depressed person feels.
• Discuss the skit using the following questions:

1. What was wrong with each visitor's approach? (Lacked understanding, assumed the depressed kid can just "snap out of it," assumed depression meant a flaw in the person's Christianity.)

2. How does the depressed person feel? (Blue, rotten, no energy, no hope, no enthusiasm.)

3. What would you want a friend to say and do if you were depressed? (Answers might include: "Stay with me," "Let me talk," "Go with me to get help," etc.)

Cast
Depressed Kid
Visitor #1
Visitor #2
Visitor #3
Time: The present
Place: Depressed Kid's home
(As skit begins, Depressed Kid is sitting on a chair in the front of the room. He's looking down, his face sad. He remains this way throughout the skit.)

Visitor #1: Hey, c'mon. We're all going to the game. (Pulls on Depressed Kid's arm.) What's the matter with you? You're no fun anymore. If that's the way you feel, we'll just go without you. (Visitor #1 leaves. Depressed Kid moves his chair a half turn to the right.)

Visitor #2: What've you got to be miserable about? Now Ted—he's got problems. Andrea dumped him, he's failing math, and he got cut from the basketball team. (Visitor #2 waves her hand in disgust and walks off. Depressed Kid moves his chair a half turn to the right.)

Visitor #3: Don't you know that good Christians don't get depressed? If you'd just pray and read your Bible, you'd be fine. I'm never depressed, and it's all because I'm a Christian. (Visitor #3 walks off, nose in the air. Depressed Kid moves his chair a half turn, so his back faces the audience.)

TEAM EFFORT—HIGH SCHOOL (10-15 Minutes)
STRESS AND MOODINESS
• Divide students into groups of three or four.
• Give each student a copy of "Stress and Moodiness" on pages 181 and 183 and a pen or pencil, or display the page using an overhead projector.
• Have students complete the page and discuss their responses.
• Stress can be a major factor in our mood swings. Listed below is a very thorough listing of causes and symptoms of stress. Read each cause and symptom and check the ones you've experienced.

IN THE WORD (25-30 Minutes)
PUT LIFE IN PERSPECTIVE
• Give each student a copy of "Put Life in Perspective" on page 185 and a pen or pencil, or display the page using an overhead projector.
• As a whole group, complete the Bible study.
1. Get out of the moodiness habit. Sometimes it is easy to be judgmental or feel sorry for ourselves. Sometimes we slip into a bad habit of getting irritated over little insignificant things. What is Paul's suggestion in Philippians 2:142? (Do everything without complaining or arguing.)
2. Put life in proper perspective.

Many people who are moody have not put God first in their lives. Read Matthew 6:25-34. What advice does Jesus give for putting life in proper perspective? (Do not worry. God knows all your needs. Seek first His kingdom and His righteousness.)
What is the result of following the advice of Jesus? (Everything will be taken care of by God.)
What areas of your life do you need to give back to God? (Students answer.)
3. Make sure there are no physical reasons for your moodiness. Physical conditions can drain us of strength and cause moodiness. Here's an easy checkup:

I get enough sleep: ☐ most of the time ☐ some of the time ☐ seldom
I eat a balanced diet: ☐ most of the time ☐ some of the time ☐ seldom
I get proper exercise: ☐ most of the time ☐ some of the time ☐ seldom
My body feels run down and tired: ☐ most of the time ☐ some of the time ☐ seldom
I have an annual physical examination: ☐ most of the time ☐ some of the time ☐ seldom

SO WHAT?
4. Work at having a positive attitude.
Are you a critical person? ☐ Yes ☐ No
Philippians 4:8 gives us good advice on developing positive attitudes. What is that advice? (To think about positive things—whatever is true, noble, right, pure, lovely, admirable, excellent and praiseworthy.)

THINGS TO THINK ABOUT (OPTIONAL)
• Use the questions on page 187 after or as a part of "In the Word."

1. Why do people not like being around a moody person?
....
....

2. Share a time when you were extremely moody and why.
....
....

3. How can you encourage a moody person?
....
....

PARENT PAGE
• Distribute page to parents.

TEAM EFFORT

NO-HELP HELPERS[1]

Cast
Depressed Kid
Visitor #1
Visitor #2
Visitor #3
Time: The present
Place: Depressed Kid's home

(As skit begins, Depressed Kid is sitting on a chair in the front of the room. He's looking down, his face sad. He remains this way throughout the skit.)

Visitor #1: Hey, c'mon. We're all going to the game. (Pulls on Depressed Kid's arm.) What's the matter with you? You're no fun anymore. If that's the way you feel, we'll just go without you. (Visitor #1 leaves. Depressed Kid moves his chair a half turn to the right.)

Visitor #2: What've you got to be miserable about? Now Ted—he's got problems. Andrea dumped him, he's failing math, and he got cut from the basketball team. (Visitor #2 waves her hand in disgust and walks off. Depressed Kid moves his chair a half turn to the right.)

Visitor #3: Don't you know that good Christians don't get depressed? If you'd just pray and read your Bible, you'd be fine. I'm never depressed, and it's all because I'm a Christian. (Visitor #3 walks off, nose in the air. Depressed Kid moves his chair a half turn, so his back faces the audience.)

Note

1. *When Kids Have Personal Problems* (Elgin, Ill.: David C. Cook Publishing, 1991), p. 13-A. Used by permission.

MOODINESS

STRESS AND MOODINESS

Stress can be a major factor in our mood swings. Listed below is a very thorough listing of causes and symptoms of stress. Read each cause and symptom and check the ones you've experienced.

Symptoms of Stress

- ☐ Aggressiveness
- ☐ Apathy
- ☐ Boredom
- ☐ Constipation
- ☐ Depression
- ☐ Dizziness
- ☐ Excessive frustration
- ☐ Habitual clearing of throat
- ☐ Hostility
- ☐ Insecurity
- ☐ Loss of confidence
- ☐ Mood swings
- ☐ Nightmares
- ☐ Pacing or wandering
- ☐ Panicky fears
- ☐ Poor concentration
- ☐ Rapid heartbeat
- ☐ Restlessness
- ☐ Self-neglect
- ☐ Silence
- ☐ Stuttering
- ☐ Tapping fingers or feet
- ☐ Tics or twitches
- ☐ Unexplained irritability
- ☐ Unusual perspiring
- ☐ Violence
- ☐ Worrying

- ☐ Anxiety
- ☐ Biting nails
- ☐ Clenching jaws
- ☐ Crying
- ☐ Diarrhea
- ☐ Eating disorders
- ☐ Grinding teeth
- ☐ Headaches
- ☐ Inattention
- ☐ Lethargy
- ☐ Loud or rapid speech
- ☐ Muscle aches
- ☐ Nit-picking
- ☐ Picking at skin or blemishes
- ☐ Persistent fatigue
- ☐ Poor self-esteem
- ☐ Rashes and other skin disorders
- ☐ Rudeness or use of shocking language
- ☐ Short-term memory loss
- ☐ Stomachaches
- ☐ Suicide thoughts, gestures or attempts
- ☐ Teary-eyedness
- ☐ Ulcers
- ☐ Unpreparedness
- ☐ Use/abuse of alcohol or other drugs
- ☐ Withdrawal

Causes of Stress

- ☐ Academic problems
- ☐ Alcohol abuse by family member(s)
- ☐ Physical and emotional changes experienced in puberty and adolescence
- ☐ Domestic violence
- ☐ Drug abuse by family member(s)
- ☐ Emotional or psychological problems of family member(s)

MOODINESS

Team Effort

- ☐ Excessive discipline by parents
- ☐ Family tensions
- ☐ Fear of failure
- ☐ Illness or death of a close friend
- ☐ Illness or death of a family member
- ☐ Inadequate housing
- ☐ Inconsistent parental discipline
- ☐ Lack of effective communication between family members
- ☐ Living in a dangerous neighborhood
- ☐ Living in a single-parent household
- ☐ Moving or changing schools
- ☐ One or both parents are frequently absent from home
- ☐ Overcrowding at home
- ☐ Parental issues
- ☐ Parental separation or divorce
- ☐ Peer pressures
- ☐ Personal health problems
- ☐ Personal setbacks, disappointments or embarrassments
- ☐ Physical deformities
- ☐ Physical or emotional neglect
- ☐ Physical, sexual or psychological abuse
- ☐ Racism
- ☐ Rejection by family members, friends, peers or others
- ☐ School or athletic performance anxieties
- ☐ Sexual impulses
- ☐ Unrealistic parental expectations or demands
- ☐ Unrealistic teacher expectations or demands

IN THE WORD

PUT LIFE IN PERSPECTIVE

1. Get out of the moodiness habit.

Sometimes it is easy to be judgmental or feel sorry for ourselves. Sometimes we slip into a bad habit of getting irritated over little insignificant things.

What is Paul's suggestion in Philippians 2:14?

....

....

2. Put life in proper perspective.

Many people who are moody have not put God first in their lives. Read Matthew 6:25-34.

What advice does Jesus give for putting life in proper perspective?

....

....

....

What is the result of following the advice of Jesus?

....

....

....

What areas of your life do you need to give back to God?

....

....

....

3. Make sure there are no physical reasons for your moodiness. Physical conditions can drain us of strength and cause moodiness. Here's an easy checkup:

I get enough sleep:	☐ most of the time	☐ some of the time	☐ seldom
I eat a balanced diet:	☐ most of the time	☐ some of the time	☐ seldom
I get proper exercise:	☐ most of the time	☐ some of the time	☐ seldom
My body feels run down and tired:	☐ most of the time	☐ some of the time	☐ seldom
I have an annual physical examination:	☐ most of the time	☐ some of the time	☐ seldom

SO WHAT?

4. Work at having a positive attitude.

Are you a critical person?

☐ Yes

☐ No

Philippians 4:8 gives us good advice on developing positive attitudes. What is that advice?

....

....

....

....

....

....

....

....

....

....

185

*T*HINGS TO THINK ABOUT

1. Why do people not like being around a moody person?

....

....

....

2. Share a time when you were extremely moody and why.

....

....

....

3. How can you encourage a moody person?

....

....

....

....

MOODINESS

PARENT PAGE

Listed below are 10 emotions moody people dwell on. All people struggle with these feelings from time to time, but a moody person may be preoccupied by one or more of them. **Read each emotion (if you don't know what it means, look it up in the dictionary) and then circle the ones that you tend to struggle with in your life.**

1. Worry
2. Anger
3. Competitiveness
4. Jealousy
5. Sulkiness

6. Inadequacy
7. Fear
8. Frustration
9. Self-pity
10. Being judgmental

Now take the words you circled and list them. Then write why you feel that these struggles are in your life (for example: Anger—I struggle with anger because of a learning disability and my parents' divorce.).

....

....

....

....

....

Family Stressors

Take some time to have each family member share their family stressors.

Rules:

1. While each family member is speaking, no one else can interrupt.

2. You can't preach or be defensive.

3. Remember that listening is the language of love.

After everyone has shared their family stressors, come up with three to five action steps to relieve a little of the stress in the family.

Action Steps:

1. ....

2. ....

3. ....

4. ....

5. ....

Session 10 "Moodiness"

Date ....

WORRY

Key Verses

"Do not be anxious about anything, but in everything, by prayer and petition, with thanksgiving, present your requests to God. And the peace of God, which transcends all understanding, will guard your hearts and your minds in Christ Jesus." Philippians 4:6,7

Biblical Basis

Psalm 139:23,24;
Proverbs 3:5,6; 17:22; 23:7;
Matthew 6:25-34;
Philippians 3:12-14; 4:6-8;
1 Thessalonians 5:18

The Big Idea

Worry takes our minds and hearts off God and cripples us from experiencing the abundant lives we can have in Jesus Christ.

Aims of This Session

During this session you will guide students to:
- Examine the worry habit in their lives;
- Discover how to overcome the crippling problem of chronic worry;
- Implement biblical principles trusting God and living with less worry.

Warm Up

How to Worry—
Common areas of concern for teens.

Team Effort— Junior High/ Middle School

What? Me Worry?—
Students examine life situations that cause worry.

Team Effort— High School

Worry-o-Meter—
Teens rate their degrees of worrying.

In the Word

You Can Fight the Worry Habit—
A Bible study on avoiding worry and trusting God.

Things to Think About (Optional)

Questions to get students thinking and talking about how worry hinders them.

Parent Page

A tool to get the session into the home and allow parents and young people to discuss avoiding worry and stress.

Leader's Devotional

"Search me, O God, and know my heart; test me and know my anxious thoughts. See if there is any offensive way in me, and lead me in the way everlasting" (Psalm 139:23,24).

I used to think I worried a lot until I met a junior high school girl who couldn't get to sleep because she worried so much. Literally speaking, this young girl was so self-conscious (like a lot of junior highers) that almost everything she thought about became a worry.

Does God really love me? Am I a good enough Christian? Do boys think I'm pretty? Am I fat? Will I ever be a really good tennis player? Is there a devil in my room? Are my grades good enough? How well will I do on my test tomorrow?

This poor girl worried so much and got so little sleep that she became exhausted at school. Her mind raced like a computer hard drive, never slowing down enough to allow her to relax and get some much needed perspective. Though she worries, worries, worries all the time, she has yet to see any of her worries come true.

This lesson will be helpful for you and your students alike. Worry is a disease of the spirit that plagues everyone. Though this life presents plenty of legitimate reasons to worry, God wants us to replace our worries with His peace.

Working with teenagers is a wonderful way to become others-centered. It's a healthy alternative to focusing on your worries. Though finances, relational problems, work conflicts, inner struggles and health concerns can sap your emotional energy by the worries that they bring, serving young people as a sign of your devotion to the Lord can bring some eternal perspective to your present circumstances. How you handle worry and anxiety provides teenagers a needed example of coping skills they may not get at home.

Before you begin this lesson today, spend some time studying Philippians 4:6,7. Present all your worries, anxieties and concerns to God. Lay everything in His hands. Praise God for His faithfulness and love for you. God promises His peace and presence to those who ask for it. (Written by Joey O'Connor.)

"Never worry about anything that is past. Charge it up to experience and forget the trouble. There are always plenty of troubles ahead, so don't turn and look back on any behind you."— Herbert Hoover

WORRY

EY VERSES

"Do not be anxious about anything, but in everything, by prayer and petition, with thanksgiving, present your requests to God. And the peace of God, which transcends all understanding, will guard your hearts and your minds in Christ Jesus." Philippians 4:6,7

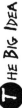IBLICAL BASIS

Psalm 139:23,24; Proverbs 3:5,6; 17:22; 23:7; Matthew 6:25-34; Philippians 3:12-14; 4:6-8; 1 Thessalonians 5:18

THE BIG IDEA

Worry takes our minds and hearts off God and cripples us from experiencing abundant lives we can have in Jesus Christ.

WARM UP (10-15 MINUTES)
HOW TO WORRY

• Give each student a copy of "How to Worry" on page 195 and a pen or pencil, or display the page using an overhead projector.
• Have students complete the page.
• As a whole group, discuss the answers.
  • Worry that if you kiss too much, you'll get mononucleosis.
  • Worry that in a long kiss, you'll have to breathe through your nose and your nose will be stopped up.
  • Worry that your breath smells.
  • Worry that you have B.O.
  • Worry that everyone is in on the joke but you.
  • Worry that if you are a girl you don't have any breasts.
  • Worry that if you are a boy you have breasts.
  • Worry that your nose is too fat. Worry that your nose is too long.
  • Worry that your neck is too fat.
  • Worry that your ears stick out.
  • Worry that your eyebrows are too close together.
  • If you are a boy, worry that you'll never be able to grow a mustache.
  • If you are a girl, worry that you have a mustache.

Fold

---

1. Yesterday is past.
Read what Paul had to say about his yesterdays in Philippians 3:12-14.
Why is this such a healthy attitude? (Students answer.)
What experience(s) in your past do you have to overcome to get a better perspective on your future? (Students answer.)

2. Your mind matters.
"For as he thinks in his heart, so is he" (Proverbs 23:7, NKJV).
How does this proverb relate to the idea of overcoming worry in your life? (Students answer.)
What is Paul's suggestion in Philippians 4:8? (Think positively.)

3. Thankful hearts are happy hearts.
What does 1 Thessalonians 5:18 say is God's will for our lives? (To give thanks in all circumstances.)
Summarize Proverbs 17:22. (Students answer.)
How can you become a more thankful person? (Students answer.)

4. Trusting in God is the opposite of worrying.
Read Proverbs 3:5,6.
What could be the result of worry? (Remember—worry is lack of trust in God.)

5. Live one day at a time.
Read Matthew 6:25-34.
What is this section of Scripture telling you not to worry about? (Anything, daily needs.)
What is the answer to worrying according to verse 33? (Seek God and His righteousness.)
Verse 34 tells us to live one day at a time. What does that mean for you? How can this biblical suggestion help your life? (Students answer.)

SO WHAT?
What worries in your life do you need to give to God?

....

THINGS TO THINK ABOUT (OPTIONAL)
• Use the questions on page 203 after or as a part of "In the Word."
1. How can worry and stress hinder you from getting day-to-day tasks completed?

....

2. How can worry and stress mess up your relationship with God?

....

3. In what ways would your life be different if you trusted God more?

....

PARENT PAGE
• Distribute page to parents.

• Worry that you won't like the food at other people's houses.
• Worry that you will eat too much food at other people's houses.
• Worry that when you go to the bathroom, people will hear. Worry that the lock on the door doesn't work.

What are other worries of teenagers? (Students answer.)

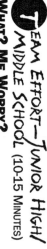

TEAM EFFORT—JUNIOR HIGH/MIDDLE SCHOOL (10-15 MINUTES)

WHAT? ME WORRY?

• Give each student a copy of "What? Me Worry?" on page 197 and a pen or pencil, or display the page using an overhead projector.
• Have students complete their pages.

Worry is something we all do. The following is a stimulating outline for a discussion on "worry."

1. Respond to these statements:
   a. Christians should never worry.
   b. Why worry?
   c. If you don't care enough to worry, you don't care.

2. List some things that you worry about.

3. List some things that your parents worry about.

4. Can you list any good consequences of worrying?

5. Can you list any bad consequences of worrying?

6. What would you say to someone who was worried about:
   a. His or her parents getting a divorce?

   b. Failing in school?

   c. Unconfessed sin?

   d. The recent loss of a boy(girl) friend?

   e. Future plans?

   f. Bad case of acne?

g. Meaningless prayer life?

h. A recent failure?

i. Death?

j. Pregnant and unmarried?

TEAM EFFORT—HIGH SCHOOL (10-15 MINUTES)

WORRY-O-METER

• Divide students into groups of three or four.
• Give each student a copy of "Worry-o-Meter" on page 199 and a pen or pencil, or display the page using an overhead projector.
• Have students complete their pages.
• Discuss answers.

Give a number to each of these potentially stressful issues (10 means "I worry about this all the time," 1 means "I've never been stressed about this a day in my life").

1. What can you do to reduce these worries?

2. Why do you think we worry even when we don't want to?

3. When do you tend to blow your worries out of perspective?

IN THE WORD (25-30 MINUTES)

YOU CAN FIGHT THE WORRY HABIT

• Give each student a copy of "You Can Fight the Worry Habit" on page 201 and a pen or pencil, or display the page using an overhead projector.
• As a whole group, complete the Bible study.

The Bible has some very practical suggestions for dealing with worry. Let's look at these suggestions and see how they can help you fight the worry habit.

 **W**ARM UP

HOW TO WORRY[1]

- Worry that if you kiss too much, you'll get mononucleosis.
- Worry that in a long kiss, you'll have to breathe through your nose and your nose will be stopped up.
- Worry that your breath smells.
- Worry that you have B.O.
- Worry that everyone is in on the joke but you.
- Worry that if you are a girl you don't have any breasts.
- Worry that if you are a boy you have breasts.
- Worry that your nose is too fat. Worry that your nose is too long.
- Worry that your neck is too fat.
- Worry that your ears stick out.
- Worry that your eyebrows are too close together.
- If you are a boy, worry that you'll never be able to grow a mustache.
- If you are a girl, worry that you have a mustache.
- Worry that you won't like the food at other people's houses.
- Worry that you will eat too much food at other people's houses.
- Worry that when you go to the bathroom, people will hear. Worry that the lock on the door doesn't work. Worry that someone will walk in.

What are other worries of teenagers?

....

....

....

....

Note

1. Mike Yaconelli, Speech delivered at the National Youth Workers Resource Seminar, Youth Specialties, Chicago 1985.
   Used by permission.

*T*EAM *EFFORT*

WHAT? ME WORRY?[1]

Worry is something we all do. The following is a stimulating outline for a discussion on "worry."

1. Respond to these statements:
    a. Christians should never worry. ....
    b. Why worry? ....
    c. If you don't care enough to worry, you don't care. ....

2. List some things that you worry about.
....

3. List some things that your parents worry about.
....

4. Can you list any good consequences of worrying?
....

5. Can you list any bad consequences of worrying?
....

6. What would you say to someone who was worried about:
    a. His or her parents getting a divorce? ....
    ....

    b. Failing in school? ....
    ....

    c. Unconfessed sin? ....
    ....

    d. The recent loss of a boy(girl) friend? ....
    ....

    e. Future plans? ....
    ....

    f. Bad case of acne? ....
    ....

    g. Meaningless prayer life? ....
    ....

    h. A recent failure? ....
    ....

    i. Death? ....
    ....

    j. Pregnant and unmarried? ....
    ....

Note

1. *Ideas Numbers 17-20* (El Cajon, Calif.: Youth Specialties, 1981), p. 150. Used by permission.

WORRY

*T*EAM *EFFORT*

WORRY-O-METER

Give a number to each of these potential stressful issues (10 means "I worry about this all the time," 1 means "I've never been stressed about this a day in my life").

Homework

Other:
....

Dating

Money

Phone

Relationship with God

Parents

Activities

Sister/brother

Grades

Friends

Clothes

1. What can you do to reduce these worries?

....
....
....

2. Why do you think we worry even when we don't want to?

....
....
....

3. When do you tend to blow your worries out of perspective?

....
....
....

IN THE WORD

YOU CAN FIGHT THE WORRY HABIT

The Bible has some very practical suggestions for dealing with worry. Let's look at these suggestions and see how they can help you fight the worry habit.

1. Yesterday is past.
Read what Paul had to say about his yesterdays in Philippians 3:12-14.
Why is this such a healthy attitude?

....

....

What experience(s) in your past do you have to overcome to get a better perspective on your future?

....

....

2. Your mind matters.
"For as he thinks in his heart, so is he" (Proverbs 23:7, *NKJV*).
How does this proverb relate to the idea of overcoming worry in your life?

....

....

What is Paul's suggestion in Philippians 4:8?

....

....

3. Thankful hearts are happy hearts.
What does 1 Thessalonians 5:18 say is God's will for our lives?

....

Summarize Proverbs 17:22. ....

....

How can you become a more thankful person?

....

....

4. Trusting in God is the opposite of worrying.
Read Proverbs 3:5,6.
What could be the result of worry? (Remember—worry is lack of trust in God.)

....

....

5. Live one day at a time.
Read Matthew 6:25-34.
What is this section of Scripture telling you not to worry about?

....

....

....

What is the answer to worrying according to verse 33?

....

....

....

Verse 34 tells us to live one day at a time. What does that mean for you? How can this biblical suggestion help your life?

....

....

....

SO WHAT?

What worries in your life do you need to give to God?

....

....

....

....

THINGS TO THINK ABOUT

1. How can worry and stress hinder you from getting day-to-day tasks completed?

....

....

....

2. How can worry and stress hinder your relationship with God?

....

....

....

3. In what ways would your life be different if you trusted God more?

....

....

....

....

PARENT PAGE

CAUTION: WORRY CAN BE HAZARDOUS TO YOUR HEALTH

Worry is a disease that is eating away the strength and faith of millions of people each and every day. The habit of worry can cripple our mental, physical and spiritual lives with the paralyzing aspect of fear. Did you know that:

- One half of the hospital beds in this country are filled with patients suffering mental and nervous disorders.
- One out of 10 people in America will suffer a complete nervous breakdown.
- Ulcers (many times caused from worry) are listed as 1 of the top 10 causes of death. High blood pressure, heart disease, headaches, thyroid problems and even the common cold can be caused from stress and worry.
- Many doctors believe that more than 80 percent of their patients could be cured if they could reduce the fears and worries in their lives.

Can you think of other problems that occur because of worry?

....

....

Here is the biblical prescription to combat worry: "Don't worry about anything; instead, pray about everything; tell God your needs and don't forget to thank him for his answers. If you do this you will experience God's peace, which is far more wonderful than the human mind can understand. His peace will keep your thoughts and your hearts quiet and at rest as you trust in Christ Jesus" (Philippians 4:6,7, *TLB*).

How will you experience God's peace?

....

What will His peace do for you?

....

....

What do you think it means to "pray about everything"?

....

....

Someone once said:
- Eighty-five percent of the things we worry about never happen;
- Ten percent of the things we worry about will happen no matter what;
- Five percent of our worries are worthwhile.

What do you think?

....

....

How can you as a family beat the worry problem?

....

....

....

....

....

....

....

....

Session 11 "Worry"

Date ....

EATING DISORDERS

KEY VERSES

"Do you not know that your body is a temple of the Holy Spirit, who is in you, whom you have received from God? You are not your own; you were bought at a price. Therefore honor God with your body." 1 Corinthians 6:19,20

BIBLICAL BASIS

1 Samuel 16:7;
Psalm 139:13-18;
Luke 12:6,7;
1 Corinthians 6:19,20

THE BIG IDEA

Many people have a problem with what and how they eat. God's plan is for us to treat our bodies as His temple.

AIMS OF THIS SESSION

During this session you will guide students to:
- Examine what an eating disorder is;
- Discover what the Bible has to say about what we do or do not put into our bodies;
- Implement healthy and godly approaches to eating.

WARM UP

ME AND FOOD—
Students share their eating habits.

TEAM EFFORT— JUNIOR HIGH/ MIDDLE SCHOOL

THE EATING QUIZ—
A look at the importance we place on food.

TEAM EFFORT— HIGH SCHOOL

SPECIAL REPORT: ANOREXIC ATHLETES—
Students examine the fatal effects of eating disorders.

IN THE WORD

KNOW THE FACTS ABOUT EATING DISORDERS—
A Bible study on God's view of the body and eating.

THINGS TO THINK ABOUT (OPTIONAL)

Questions to get students thinking and talking about eating disorders.

PARENT PAGE

A tool to get the session into the home and allow parents and young people to discuss family eating habits.

LEADER'S DEVOTIONAL

"Are not five sparrows sold for two pennies? Yet not one of them is forgotten by God. Indeed, the very hairs of your head are all numbered. Don't be afraid; you are worth more than many sparrows" (Luke 12:6,7).

As roommates during our freshman year in college, Tom and I frequently went to the school cafeteria together. It wasn't until our sophomore year, however, that I noticed that Tom was becoming unusually thin. I wasn't the only one who noticed either.

One day, on my way back from class, I bumped into Tom and asked where he was headed. His response wasn't what I expected.

"I just met with the dean and he told me my parents were coming to take me to a hospital. They say I have an eating disorder."

Tom was skinnier than usual, but I didn't realize how bad his physical and emotional condition really was. At 6'2", Tom was a mere 105 pounds. Though he didn't realize it, he was literally starving himself to death.

Tom wasn't the first person I'd known with an eating disorder. Over the past few years, I've spoken with numerous guys and girls about their struggles with overeating, bulimia and anorexia. Eating disorders are an insidious evil that ravage the body and spirit. Dealing with teenagers who struggle with eating disorders is a long-term process. Your unconditional love and support provide them the mirror image of God's grace.

If you wrestle with your eating habits or self-image, know that you are fearfully and wonderfully made. You are a precious creation designed by the wonderful hands of God. Regardless if you have trouble with an eating disorder or not, nothing can change His love for you. You are His child and you can take comfort in His compassion for you. Let your self-image rest in God's image. In His eyes, you are a masterpiece! (Written by Joey O'Connor.)

"Pain is an energy monster; we give it the power to hurt us. And we can take that power away—depending on how we choose to view ourselves. All pain is real, but you can change your reality."—David Black

EATING DISORDERS

KEY VERSES

"Do you not know that your body is a temple of the Holy Spirit, who is in you, whom you have received from God? You are not your own; you were bought at a price. Therefore honor God with your body." 1 Corinthians 6:19,20

BIBLICAL BASIS

1 Samuel 16:7; Psalm 139:13-18; Luke 12:6,7; 1 Corinthians 6:19,20

THE BIG IDEA

Many people have a problem with what and how they eat. God's plan is for us to treat our bodies as His temple.

WARM UP (10-15 MINUTES)

ME AND FOOD

- Divide students into groups of three or four.
- Have students complete the following statements:
  My favorite food is:
  The most unique meal I've ever had is:
  My favorite restaurant is:
  My favorite fast food is:
  My favorite candy is:
  The food I hate most is:

TEAM EFFORT—JUNIOR HIGH/ MIDDLE SCHOOL (10-15 MINUTES)

THE EATING QUIZ

- Give each student a copy of "The Eating Quiz" on page 211 and a pen or pencil, or display the page using an overhead projector.
- Have students complete the page.

--- Fold ---

209

How does this Scripture relate to our eating habits? (Students answer.)

Why do you think we as Christians are much more lenient on what we put into or do to our bodies than on other sins? (Students answer.)

Our Looks: "But the Lord said to Samuel, 'Do not consider his appearance or his height, for I have rejected him. The Lord does not look at the things man looks at the outward appearance, but the Lord looks at the heart'" (1 Samuel 16:7).

What makes this Scripture sound like it could have been written just last week? (Students answer.)

Why is it difficult to accept inner beauty over outer beauty? (Students answer.)

Our Beings: "For you created my inmost being; you knit me together in my mother's womb. I praise you because I am fearfully and wonderfully made; your works are wonderful, I know that full well. My frame was not hidden from you when I was made in the secret place. When I was woven together in the depths of the earth, your eyes saw my unformed body. All the days ordained for me were written in your book before one of them came to be. How precious to me are your thoughts, O God! How vast is the sum of them! Were I to count them, they would outnumber the grains of sand. When I awake, I am still with you" (Psalm 139:13-18).

How could you use this Scripture to comfort a person with an eating disorder? (Students answer.)

Circle the words in this psalm that have something to do with God creating us. Then discuss these words as a group.

SO WHAT?

After you've looked at the facts of eating disorders and read these Scriptures, what decisions do you need to make to treat better your "temple of God"?

....

....

THINGS TO THINK ABOUT (OPTIONAL)

- Use the questions on page 221 after or as a part of "In the Word."

1. Can you name any famous people who had eating disorders? What were the outcomes of their problems?

....

....

2. Why is our society obsessed with thin, sleek bodies?

....

....

3. What advice would you give to a friend who has an eating disorder?

....

....

PARENT PAGE

- Distribute page to parents.

• Explain that the correct answer to every question is d. Then ask:

What does this quiz say about our society?

Share the following: A missionary who had served in several countries over many years made a curious observation on a return trip to the United States. "In all the places I've visited, all the people I've met think they have to eat in order to live. But here in America, almost everyone I know thinks they live in order to eat! You people spend more time talking about food, planning meals and preparing snacks than anyone else in the world."

Ask volunteers to respond to the missionary's statement.

1. On the average, Americans spend as much money on between-meal snacks as they do on which meal?
a. Breakfast
b. Lunch
c. Dinner
d. All of the above

2. In a recent survey, couples planning weddings said their biggest concern was:
a. Where to go on their honeymoon
b. How many people to invite to the ceremony
c. What time to hold the wedding
d. What food to serve at the reception

3. More advertising dollars are spent on this product than any others.
a. Automobiles
b. Computers
c. Clothing
d. Snack food and beverages

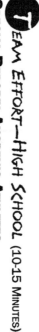

TEAM EFFORT—HIGH SCHOOL (10-15 Minutes)

SPECIAL REPORT: ANOREXIC ATHLETES

• Divide students into groups of three or four.
• Give each student a copy of "Special Report: Anorexic Athletes" on page 213 and a pen or pencil, or display the page using an overhead projector.
• Have students complete their pages.

The recent death of U.S. gymnast Christy Henrich due to complications from anorexia nervosa has again pushed eating disorders to the forefront of many health and psychology discussions.

Henrich, who weighed a pitiful 47 pounds at one point in her illness, is only one of many marquee athletes and performers who have recently battled with eating disorders: Cathy Rigby, Kristine Phillips (a *Sports Illustrated* cover girl), Nadia Comaneci, Tracy Gold ("Growing Pains"), and others.

While many experts believe that the number of people with eating disorders is diminishing, they still agree current rates are at epidemic proportions. According to the National Association of Anorexia Nervosa and Associated Disorders, an estimated eight million in the U.S. alone suffer from eating disorders. Among these, an estimated 3% to 6% of the more serious cases will die each year.

All experts agree that low self-esteem, poor body image, and a history of family perfectionism are big factors in determining a girl's susceptibility to eating disorders. For example, eating disorders can be very common on Christian campuses, points out a counselor at Rosemead School of Psychology in Southern California. In fact, they are among the more acceptable disorders among the Christian community as a whole.

Fold

Eating disorders are very real, very common problems in many youth groups. "A girl in my club told me she falls into a binge-and-purge cycle every time things get rough at home," says a female volunteer youth worker in northern Minnesota. "Another girl, who graduated last June, fought eating disorders since her sophomore year, and ended up being hospitalized before recovering."

Why do you suppose athletes are more susceptible to eating disorders than other people?

This article says that eating disorders are very common on Christian college campuses and are more accepted than other problems. Do you think this is true? If so, why?

All experts agree that low self-esteem, poor body image and a history of family perfectionism are all factors in determining a person's susceptibility to having an eating disorder. Why do you think these three factors make such an impact?

IN THE WORD (25-30 Minutes)

KNOW THE FACTS ABOUT EATING DISORDERS

• Divide students into groups of three or four.
• Give each student a copy of "Know the Facts About Eating Disorders" on pages 215, 217, 219 and 221 and a pen or pencil, or display the page using an overhead projector.
• As a whole group, complete the Bible study.

Eating disorders can occur for a variety of reasons. There is almost always a root cause or causes. Many eating disorders stem from poor views of self and body, family perfectionism or sexual abuse.

Anne with Anorexia
Anne is obsessed with being thin. She deliberately "starves herself." Anorexia nervosa literally means "loss of appetite because of nerves." Because she is not in the later stages, Anne feels hungry. She chooses not to eat. Even though she is extremely thin, she still believes she is fat. Anne is a gymnast and is consumed with exercise, her body and keeping thin. She hides the fact that she doesn't eat much and has used laxatives to "help keep her weight down." Anne is a perfectionist. If Anne doesn't get help and she keeps losing weight, her obsession to starve could be fatal.

Bonnie with Bulimia
Bonnie is a binge eater. She will eat huge amounts of food at one sitting. One day she ate a whole half gallon of ice cream and a cake! Then she will often purge the food by vomiting, abusing laxatives or taking diuretics. Bulimia literally means "ox hunger." Bonnie doesn't eat because of overwhelming hunger, but because of stress, depression, loneliness, anger, frustration or other problems in her life. If she continues her behavior, she could develop physical problems with her colon, kidney and digestive systems; very dry skin; body chemical imbalances; light-headedness and bloating.

Craig with a Compulsive Eating Disorder
When Craig is under a lot of stress he eats. Craig eats for emotional reasons—when he's depressed or feeling guilty. Unlike his friend Bonnie the Bulimic, he doesn't try to purge the food. He is often on a diet, but as soon as something goes wrong he doesn't just eat half a donut, he eats five whole donuts. He is munching on potato chips or something all the time. Consequently he is overweight. His overeating satisfies an emotional rather than physical hunger.

How Should We Treat Our Bodies?
Our Bodies: "Do you not know that your body is a temple of the Holy Spirit, who is in you, whom you have received from God? You are not your own; you were bought at a price. Therefore honor God with your body" (I Corinthians 6:19,20).

THE EATING QUIZ[1]

1. On the average, Americans spend as much money on between-meal snacks as they do on which meal?
   a. Breakfast
   b. Lunch
   c. Dinner
   d. All of the above

2. In a recent survey, couples planning weddings said their biggest concern was:
   a. Where to go on their honeymoon
   b. How many people to invite to the ceremony
   c. What time to hold the wedding
   d. What food to serve at the reception

3. More advertising dollars are spent on this product than any others.
   a. Automobiles
   b. Computers
   c. Clothing
   d. Snack food and beverages

Note

1. Adapted from *When Kids Have Personal Problems* (Elgin, Ill.: David C. Cook Publishing Co., 1991), p. 58.
   Used by permission.

EATING
DISORDERS

SPECIAL REPORT: ANOREXIC ATHLETES[1]

The recent death of U.S. gymnast Christy Henrich due to complications from anorexia nervosa has again pushed eating disorders to the forefront of many health and psychology discussions.

Henrich, who weighed a pitiful 47 pounds at one point in her illness, is only one of many marquee athletes and performers who have recently battled with eating disorders: Cathy Rigby, Kristine Phillips (a *Sports Illustrated* cover girl), Nadia Comaneci, Tracy Gold ("Growing Pains"), and others.

While many experts believe that the number of people with eating disorders is diminishing, they still agree current rates are at epidemic proportions. According to the National Association of Anorexia Nervosa and Associated Disorders, an estimated eight million in the U.S. alone suffer from eating disorders. Among these, an estimated 3% to 6% of the more serious cases will die each year.

All experts agree that low self-esteem, poor body image, and a history of family perfectionism are big factors in determining a girl's susceptibility to eating disorders. For example, eating disorders can be very common on Christian campuses, points out a counselor at Rosemead School of Psychology in Southern California. In fact, they are among the more acceptable disorders among the Christian community as a whole.

Eating disorders are very real, very common problems in many youth groups. "A girl in my club told me she falls into a binge-and-purge cycle every time things get rough at home," says a female volunteer youth worker in northern Minnesota. "Another girl, who graduated last June, fought eating disorders since her sophomore year, and ended up being hospitalized before recovering."

Why do you suppose athletes are more susceptible to eating disorders than other people?

....

....

This article says that eating disorders are very common on Christian college campuses and are more accepted than other problems. Do you think this is true? If so, why?

....

....

All experts agree that low self-esteem, poor body image and a history of family perfectionism are all factors in determining a person's susceptibility to having an eating disorder. Why do you think these three factors make such an impact?

....

....

....

Note

1. "Anorexic Athletes," *Youth Worker Update*,
   October 1994. Used by permission.

EATING DISORDERS

IN THE WORD

KNOW THE FACTS ABOUT EATING DISORDERS

Eating disorders can occur for a variety of reasons. There is almost always a root cause or causes. Many eating disorders stem from poor views of self and body, family perfectionism or sexual abuse.

Anne with Anorexia

Anne is obsessed with being thin. She deliberately "starves herself." Anorexia nervosa literally means "loss of appetite because of nerves." Because she is not in the later stages, Anne feels hungry. She chooses not to eat. Even though she is extremely thin, she still believes she is fat. Anne is a gymnast and is consumed with exercise, her body and keeping thin. She hides the fact that she doesn't eat much and has used laxatives to "help keep her weight down." Anne is a perfectionist. If Anne doesn't get help and she keeps losing weight, her obsession to starve could be fatal.

Symptoms of Anorexia Nervosa[1]
• Dramatic weight loss with no evident physical illness
• Excessive exercise
• Feeling "fat" when not obese
• Preoccupation with food, calories, nutrition or cooking
• Refusal to eat or eating only small amounts
• Thinness to the point of emaciation
• Loss of menstrual period
• Hunger denial
• Distorted body image
• Binge-eating
• Abuse of laxatives or diuretics
• Forced vomiting after eating
• Strange food obsessions and rituals
• Frequent weighing
• Fear, approaching phobia, of being fat, even when quite thin
• Oversensitive to criticism
• Perfectionism
• Extremely controlled behavior
• Intolerance of others' imperfections as well as her own
• Hyperactivity
• Unusual dedication to one activity
• Reluctance to express anger

Bonnie with Bulimia

Bonnie is a binge eater. She will eat huge amounts of food at one sitting. One day she ate a whole half gallon of ice cream and a cake! Then she will often purge the food by vomiting, abusing laxatives or taking diuretics. Bulimia literally means "ox hunger." Bonnie doesn't eat because of over-

EATING
DISORDERS

IN THE WORD

whelming hunger, but because of stress, depression, loneliness, anger, frustration or other problems in her life. If she continues her behavior, she could develop physical problems with her colon, kidney and digestive systems; very dry skin; body chemical imbalances; light-headedness and bloating.

Symptoms of Bulimia[2]
• Alcohol abuse or dependency
• Addictive behavior
• Depression and mood swings
• Dental problems
• Disappearing after meals
• Displaying excessive concern about weight
• Drug abuse or dependency
• Emotional instability or impulsivity
• Excessive exercise to control weight
• Fear of weight gain (especially when the person is within 15 pounds of their normal body weight)
• Feeling guilty about eating
• Feeling out-of-control
• Frequent weight fluctuations
• Inability to stop the binge/purge cycle
• Overeating, especially when distressed
• Planning binges or seeking opportunities to binge
• Preoccupation with food, calories or nutrition
• Restrictive diets followed by food binges, especially with high-calorie sweets
• Secretive about binges and/or purging
• Sexual fears
• Swelling of the parotid glands (at the jaw line)
• Throat, esophagus, stomach or colon problems
• Water retention and swelling of the extremities

Craig with a Compulsive Eating Disorder
When Craig is under a lot of stress he eats. Craig eats for emotional reasons—when he's depressed or feeling guilty. Unlike his friend Bonnie the Bulimic, he doesn't try to purge the food. He is often on a diet but as soon as something goes wrong he doesn't just eat half a donut, he eats five whole donuts. He is munching on potato chips or something all the time. Consequently he is overweight. His overeating satisfies an emotional rather than physical hunger.

IN THE WORD

Symptoms of Compulsive Overeating[3]
- Alternating between compulsive overeating and chronic dieting
- Binging without purging
- Eating for emotional reasons rather than hunger
- Feeling out-of-control with food
- Guilt feelings
- Low self-esteem
- Self hate

How Should We Treat Our Bodies?

Our Bodies: "Do you not know that your body is a temple of the Holy Spirit, who is in you, whom you have received from God? You are not your own; you were bought at a price. Therefore honor God with your body" (1 Corinthians 6:19,20).

How does this Scripture relate to our eating habits?

....

....

Why do you think we as Christians are much more lenient on what we put into or do to our bodies than on other sins?

....

....

Our Looks: "But the Lord said to Samuel, 'Do not consider his appearance or his height, for I have rejected him. The Lord does not look at the things man looks at. Man looks at the outward appearance, but the Lord looks at the heart'" (1 Samuel 16:7).

What makes this Scripture sound like it could have been written just last week?

....

....

....

Why is it difficult to accept inner beauty over outer beauty?

....

....

Our Beings: "For you created my inmost being; you knit me together in my mother's womb. I praise you because I am fearfully and wonderfully made; your works are wonderful, I know that full well. My frame was not hidden from you when I was made in the secret place. When I was woven together in the depths of the earth, your eyes saw my unformed body. All the days ordained for me were written in your book before one of them came to be. How precious to me are your thoughts, O God! How vast is the sum of them! Were I to count them, they would out-number the grains of sand. When I awake, I am still with you" (Psalm 139:13-18).

IN THE WORD

How could you use this Scripture to comfort a person with an eating disorder?

....

....

Circle the words in this psalm that have something to do with God creating us. Then discuss these words as a group.

SO WHAT?

After you've looked at the facts of eating disorders and read these Scriptures, what decisions do you need to make to treat better your "temple of God"?

....

....

....

Notes

1. *Childhood Eating Disorders* (Huntington, N.Y.: William Gladden Foundation, 1990), p. 14. Used by permission.

2. Ibid., p. 15.

3. Ibid.

THINGS TO THINK ABOUT

1. Can you name any famous people who had eating disorders? What were the outcomes of their problems?

....

....

2. Why is our society obsessed with thin, sleek bodies?

....

....

3. What advice would you give to a friend who has an eating disorder?

....

....

EATING DISORDERS

PARENT PAGE

EATING DISORDERS

The seven major warning signs of an eating disorder, according to the National Institute of Mental Health are:

1. You often eat what others would consider abnormally large amounts of food.
2. You are unable to control what or how much you eat.
3. You eat more rapidly than usual.
4. You eat until you're uncomfortably full.
5. You eat even when you're not hungry.
6. You eat alone because you don't want anyone to know how much you consume.
7. You feel guilty, depressed or disgusted after you've eaten too much—or even if you have eaten practically nothing at all.

"Do you not know that your body is a temple of the Holy Spirit, who is in you, whom you have received from God? You are not your own; you were bought at a price. Therefore honor God with your body" (1 Corinthians 6:19,20).

A Family Eating Habits Checkup

Yes	No	
....	....	Do you eat healthy?
....	....	Do you keep your bodies in physical shape?
....	....	Does anyone in your family display any of the major signs of an eating
....		disorder shown above?
....	....	How serious do you take the above Scripture in your family?

ACTION STEPS:

What steps can you as a family or individuals within the family take to be better stewards of your temples of God?

....

....

....

Session 12 "Eating Disorders"

Date...

Add a New Member to Your Youth Staff.

Meet Jim Burns. He won't play guitar and he doesn't do windows, but he will take care of your programming needs. That's because his new curriculum, **YouthBuilders Group Bible Studies** is a comprehensive program designed to take your group through their high school years. (If you have junior high kids in your group, **YouthBuilders** works for them too.)

For less than $6 a month you'll get Jim Burns's special recipe of high-involvement, discussion-oriented, Bible-centered studies. It's the next generation of Bible curriculum for youth—and with Jim on your staff, you'll be free to spend more time one-on-one with the kids in your group.

...rns is
...nt of the
...al
...te of
...Ministry.

Here are some of YouthBuilders' hottest features:

- Reproducible pages—one book fits your whole group

- Wide appeal—big groups, small groups—even adjusts to fit jr. high/high school groups

- Hits home—special section to involve parents with every session of the study

- Interactive Bible discovery—geared to help young people find answers themselves

- Cheat sheets—a Bible *Tuck-In*™ with all the session information on a single page

- Flexible format—perfect for Sunday mornings, midweek youth meetings, or camps and retreats

- Three studies in one—each study has three, four-session modules examining critical life choices.

   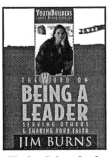 

...rd on Sex, Drugs & ...Roll
...uth a biblical framework
...ng good choices in life.
307.16424

The Word on Prayer and the Devotional Life
Help high school youth get closer to God by getting a grip on prayer. ISBN 08307.16432

The Word on the Basics of Christianity
Here are the foundational truths of Christianity, presented in an active format. ISBN 08307.16440

The Word on Being a Leader, Serving Others & Sharing Your Faith
Students can serve God and each other by taking an active role in leadership. ISBN 08307.16459

The Word on Helping Friends in Crisis
Young people can discover what God's Word says about crisis issues and how to help others. ISBN 08307.16467

Push-Button Course for Junior High.

...r. High Builders are all-in-one programs that help kids put their faith in action. Each book in the series includes 13 Bible studies, dozens of games and activities as well as clip art to illustrate your handouts—all you have to do is warm up the copier!

...h Builders titles include:
...tian Basics (ISBN 08307.16963)
...tian Relationships (ISBN 08307.17013)
...ols of Christ (ISBN 08307.17021)
...r of God (ISBN 08307.17048)
...in Action (ISBN 08307.17056)
..., Love and Truth (ISBN 08307.17064)
...yles of the Not-so-Famous from the Bible (ISBN 08307.17099)

...are only a few of the YouthBuilders and Jr. High Builders studies
...ble. For a complete list, contact your Gospel Light supplier.

Gospel Light

Youth Ministry Resources from Gospel Light.

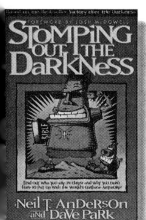

Give Your Young People the Victory.

Here is the powerful message of Neil Anderson's best-selling book, *Victory over the Darkness*, written especially for young people. *Stomping Out the Darkness* provides junior high through high school youth with the keys they are desperately searching for—keys to their identities, worth, significance, security and acceptance as children of God.

Stomping Out the Darkness
Neil Anderson and Dave Park
Trade • ISBN 08307.16408

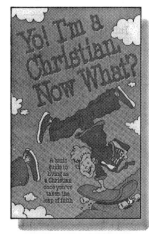

A Fun Way to Put Faith into Action.

Get young Christians off to a great start with this 10-session introduction to Christian growth cleverly disguised as a comic book. Here are dozens of games, puzzles and mazes interwoven with six daily Scripture readings and rock-solid teaching to help kids ages 10 to 15 build mature relationships with Christ.

Yo! I'm a Christian, Now What?
Rick Bundschuh and Tom Finley
Trade • ISBN 08307.14669

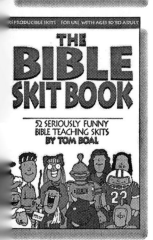

Bible Skits for All Occasions.

Here's a great way to get your kids out of their seats and into the Word. *The Bible Skit Book* gives you 52 lively, reproducible Bible-theme skits. Each skit includes director's tips, accurate Bible background information and group discussion questions. Great for camps, clubs and sermon illustrations, too. Less than 33¢ per skit!

The Bible Skit Book
Tom Boal
Manual • ISBN 08307.16238

A Support Group for Parents of Teens.

This seven-session course focuses on biblical principles of parenting, and explains seven building blocks to becoming an effective parent.

"Hi, I'm Bob and I'm the Parent of a Teenager."
Tim Smith
Manual • ISBN 08307.14650

Faster than a Speeding Bulletin.

Break through solid walls of boredom to reach youth with this fun, new, high-quality clip art that will supercharge flyers and newsletters. Here are borders, mastheads and illustrations for everything from camping, games and summer events to worship and missions activities.

Super Clip Art for Youth Workers
Tom Finley
Manual • ISBN 08307.15177

Now available for your computer!
For IBM or Mac

Ask Your Students the Questions that "Hit Home".

Fifty true case studies, compiled by Jim Burns, pose real-life moral questions to teenagers for group discussion and learning. Scripture references and discussion questions included.

The Youth Worker's Book of Case Studies
Jim Burns
Manual • ISBN 08307.15827

Gospel Light